MOTIVATION THEORIES
AND
TEACHING PROFESSION IN INDIA

MOTIVATION THEORIES
AND
TEACHING PROFESSION IN INDIA

Dr. Amarja Nargunde

PARTRIDGE
A Penguin Company

Partridge books may be ordered through booksellers or by contacting:

Partridge India
Penguin Books India Pvt.Ltd
11, Community Centre, Panchsheel Park, New Delhi 110017
India
www.partridgepublishing.com
Phone: 000.800.10062.62

CONTENTS

Dedicated To
Lord Shani Maharaj,
The Cause of
My Faith and Devotion

To Whom
I Shall Always Remain Grateful
For the Very Existence
Of My Life

ACKNOWLEDGMENT

As this book is an extension of my Ph. D. research, at the very outset I acknowledge and express my thanks to my PhD guide Dr. S.S. Sahasrabudhe and co-guide Dr. V.M.Chavan. Both of them are very renowned and well known personalities in the field academics and it was my real fortune that they guided me in my research.

This book is on motivation. I would like to acknowledge a personality who unfortunately is no more in this world. He is motivation of my life, whose life I find truly inspiring. He is late Steve Jobs, co-founder and former Apple CEO. His words "Have the courage to follow your heart and intuition . . ." motivated me to convert my writings in a book form.

Finally, I thank the divine power of Lord Shani Maharaj, Shri Aurobindo and The Mother for giving me strength to contribute my efforts in the field of knowledge and education.

PREFACE

Many authors have pointed out the real problem with education is not that of money, resources, or infrastructural facility. But it is the human mind that is in charge of passing on knowledge to the students viz. the teachers. Teachers today lack motivation. Many authors have highlighted this fact. The authors also point out that teachers themselves acknowledge that they lack motivation which has led to fall in quality of education. International Labour Organization (ILO, 1990) report lamented that the motivation of teachers had reached an intolerable low point.

I carried out my PhD research on motivation of teachers in higher education field in India. I came across different theories of motivation in different books. I have made analysis of these theories especially regarding teaching profession in colleges in India. I have pointed out why some theories have got relevance for the teaching profession and what are the difficulties in applying these theories to the profession of college teaching. I have also pointed out how some of the existing motivators can be applied to teachers. The comments are given based on the study of elaborate literature review of various articles and books written by eminent educationists on the state of college education. Since I am working in the same profession, it has also helped me in having more insight of the profession.

At the end, I have also suggested my own theory in order to motivate teachers.

1 MOTIVATION—A THEORETICAL CONCEPT

The Meaning of Motivation

In the field of Organizational Behavior, motivation is the most researched and studied topic and the research papers which are published in Organization Behavior, 80% of them are attributed to the subject of motivation.

Usually one or more of the following words are included while defining motivation: desires, wants, wishes, aims, goals, needs, motives and incentives. Technically the term motivation can be traced to the Latin word movere, which means "to move." This meaning is evident in the following comprehensive definition:

"Motivation is a process that starts with a physiological or psychological or need that activates a behavior or a drive that is aimed at a goal or incentive"

Thus, the key to understanding the process of motivation lies in the meaning of and relationships among, needs, drives and incentives.

Figures 1.1 graphically depicts the motivation process. Needs set up drive aimed at incentives; this is what the basic process of motivation is all about. In a systems sense, motivation consists of these three interacting and interdependent elements:

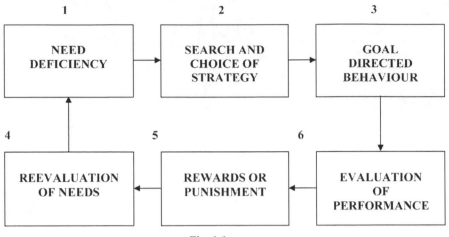

Fig. 1.1

Motivational Model

1. Needs:

Needs are created whenever there is a physiological or psychological imbalance. For example, a need exists when cells in the body are deprived of food and water or when the personality is deprived of other people who serve as friends or companions.

2. Drives:

A physiological drive can be simply defined as a deficiency with direction. Physiological and psychological drives are action oriented and provide an energizing thrust towards reaching an incentive. They are at the very heart of the motivational process.

3. Incentives:

At the end of the motivation cycle is the incentive, defined as anything that will alleviate a need and reduce a drive. Thus, attaining an incentive will tend to restore physiological or psychological balance and will reduce or cut off the drive.

Importance of Motivation

The increased attention towards motivation is justified by several reasons.

- Motivated employees are always looking for better ways to do a job.
- Motivated employees generally are more quality oriented.
- Highly motivated workers are more productive than apathetic workers. E.g. Mumbai Dubbawalas are always a matter of curiosity for management researchers across the world for their efficient services.
- Every organization requires human resources in addition to the need for financial and physical resources for it to function. Three behavioral dimensions of human resource are significant to the organization:

  (1) People must be attracted not only to join the organization but also to remain in it.
  (2) People must perform the tasks for which they are hired and must do so in a dependable manner.
  (3) People must go beyond this dependable role performance and engage in some form of creative, spontaneous and innovative behavior at work.

  In other words, for an organization to be effective, it must come to grips with the motivational problems of stimulating both the decision to participate and the decision to produce at work.

- A comprehensive understanding of the way in which organization functions requires that increasing attention be directed towards the question of why people behave as they do on their jobs. It is essential to understand how different variables like leadership style, group dynamics and compensation system affect the end results like employee performance and job satisfaction.
- As technology increases in complexity, machines tend to become necessary yet insufficient vehicles of effective and efficient operations. Modern technology can no longer be considered synonymous with the tem "automation". Millions and billions of dollars in R & D will be useless if the employees are not motivated. For example, at one point of time IBM was spending

huge money in R &D compared Apple Inc. But Apple could make dent in the market with innovative products one after the other with its motivated workforce.

- Motivation brings employees closer to organization. The needs of employees are met and employees begin to take more interest in organizational work. Motivated people are not resistant to the changes taken into the organizations. With the help of effectively motivated workforce, those changes will be accepted, introduced and implemented without negative attitude and the organization will be kept on the right track of progress. More concern is being directed in addition, towards stimulating employees to enlarge their job skills (through training, job design, job relation and so on) at both blue-collar and white collar levels in an effort to ensure a continual reservoir of well-trained and highly motivated people.

- Finally, attention paid to motivation by managers speaks about its importance in management of human resources. The more motivated the employees are, the more empowered the team is. The more is the team work and individual employee contribution, more profitable and successful is the business. Motivation leads to an optimistic and challenging attitude at work place.

Teachers and Motivation

Importance of motivation is even more for the field of teaching profession which is called as "the mother of all profession". In earlier times teaching profession and the teacher enjoyed quite high status in the society. Teachers performed without being bothered about materialistic returns. In recent times however, one has found deterioration in the quality in the field of education and apathy on the part of teachers to comply their duties with the best of their abilities. The teachers today are accused of running behind money, even using some unscrupulous means. There is complete lack of motivation for performing their duties honestly. The teachers attribute the reasons to many things including that they are the part of the society where the moral and ethical standards have gone down in the society itself, expecting teachers would remain untouched by it, is too unrealistic to believe. Like in most other professions like doctors, engineers intend to make money, what's wrong if a teacher does the same, a teacher would ask.

PRIMARY MOTIVES

These motives are also known as physiological, biological, unlearned or primary. The last term is used here because it is more comprehensive than the others. Most commonly recognized primary motives include hunger, thirst, sleep, avoidance of pain, sex and maternal concern. Two criteria must be met in order for a motive to be included in the primary classification: It must be unlearned and it must be physiologically based. However, the use of the term primary does not imply that these motives always take precedence over general and secondary motives. Although the precedence of primary motives is implied in some motivation theories, there are many situations in which general and secondary motives predominate over primary motives. Common examples are celibacy among priests and fasting for a religious, social or political cause. In both cases, learned secondary motives are stronger than unlearned primary motives.

GENERAL MOTIVES

To be included in the general category, a motive must be unlearned but not physiologically based. Whereas the primary needs seek to reduce the tension or stimulation, these general needs induce the person to increase the amount of stimulation. Thus, these needs are sometimes called "stimulus motives." Although not all psychologists would agree, the motives of curiosity, manipulation, activity and possibly affection seem best to meet the criteria for this classification.

The Curiosity, Manipulation and Activity Motives

It is generally recognized that human curiosity, manipulation and activity drives are quite intense. If these motives are stifled or inhibited, the total society might become very stagnant. The same is true on an organizational level. If employees are not allowed to explore their curiosity, manipulation and activity motives, they may not be motivated.

In case of teachers especially this becomes even truer. They want autonomy in their work, finding out answers to some of the unsolved intellectual problems through research work and exploring the knowledge world. If they are tied to routine job of taking lectures that too with heavy workload, on the class of students who hardly care for gaining knowledge but are more concerned for degree certificates, one can't blame teachers for lack of motivation.

The Affection Motive

Love or affection is a very complex form of general drive. Part of the complexity stems from the fact that in many ways love resembles the primary drives and in other ways it is similar to the secondary drives. In particular, the affection motive is closely associated with the primary sex motive on the hand and with the secondary affiliation motive on the other. For this reason, affection is sometimes placed in all three categories of motives and some psychologists do not even recognize it as a separate motive.

SECONDARY MOTIVES

Whereas the general drive seems relatively more important than the primary ones to the study of humans in organizations, the secondary drives are unquestionably the most important. As a human society develops economically and becomes more complex, the primary drives and to a lesser the general drives, give way to the learned secondary drives in motivating behavior. With some glaring exceptions that have yet to be eradicated, the motives of hunger and thirst are not dominant among people living in the economically developed world. This situation is obviously subject to change; for example, the "population bomb," nuclear war, or the greenhouse effect may alter certain human needs and further breakthroughs in neuropsychology may receive more deserved attention. But for now, the learned secondary motives dominate the study and application of the field organizational behavior.

A motive must be learned in order to be included in the secondary classification. Numerous important human motives meet this criterion. Some of the more important ones are power, achievement and affiliation or as they are commonly referred to today, nPow, nAch, nAff. In addition, especially in reference to organizational behavior, security and status are important secondary motives.

The Power of Motive

The leading advocate of the power motive was the pioneering psychologist Alfred Adler. Adler officially broke his close ties with Sigmund Freud and proposed an apposing theoretical. Whereas Freud stressed the impact of the past and of sexual, unconscious motivation, Adler substituted the future and a person's overwhelming drive for superiority or power.

To explain the power need—the need to manipulate others or the drive for being in charge of others—Adler developed the concepts of inferiority complex and compensation. He felt that every kid experiences a sense of inferiority. When this feeling of inferiority is combined with what he sensed as an innate (inborn) need for superiority, two rule all behavior. The person's lifestyle is characterized by striving to compensate for feelings of inferiority, which are combined with the innate drive for power.

There is a distinction to be made between social power and personal power. Social power, which is often a characteristic of effective leaders, is devoted to developing trust and respect from followers and is in conjunction with the leader's vision.

Although modern psychologists do not generally accept the tenet that the power drive is inborn and thus dominant in recent years, it has prompted renewed interest. The politician is probably the best example and political scandals make a fascinating study of the striving for and the use of power in government and politics. However, in addition to politicians, anyone holding a responsible position in business, government, unions, education or the military may also exhibit a considerable need for power.

The Achievement Motive

More is known about achievement than about any other motive because of the tremendous amount of research that has been devoted to it over the years. Achievement may be defined as "the degree to which a person wishes to accomplish challenging goals, success in competitive situations and exhibit the desire for unambiguous feedback regarding performance". An individual with a high need for achievement has higher of each element of the definition.

The Thematic Apperception Test (TAT) has proven to be a very effective tool in researching achievement. The TAT can effectively identify and measure the achievement motive. David C. McClelland, a recently deceased Harvard psychologist is most closely associated with study of the achievement motive. The derived specific characteristics of high achievers are summarized in the following sections.

Moderate Risk Taking

On the surface it would seem that a high achiever would take high risks. Taking moderate risks is probably the single most descriptive characteristic of the person possessing high nAch.

Need for Immediate Feedback

Closely connected to high achievers is their desire for immediate feedback. People with high nAch prefer activities that provide immediate and precise feedback information on how they are progressing towards their goals.

Satisfaction with Accomplishments

High achievers find accomplishing a task intrinsically satisfying. They do not expect or necessarily want the accompanying material rewards. A good illustration of this characteristic involves money. But not for the usual reasons of wanting money for its own sake or for the material benefits that it can buy. Rather, high nAch people look at money as a form of feedback or measurement of how they are doing. Given the choice between a simple task with a good payoff for accomplishment and a more difficult task with a lesser payoff, other things being equal, high achievers may choose the latter.

Preoccupation with the Task

Once high achievers select goals, they tend to be totally preoccupied with their tasks until they are successfully completed. They cannot stand to leave a job half finished and are not satisfied with themselves until they have given their maximum effort. This type of dedicated commitment is often reflected in their outward personalities, which frequently have negative effects on those who come into contact with them. High achievers often strike others as being unfriendly and as "loners." They may be very quiet and may seldom brag about their accomplishments. They tend to be very realistic about their abilities and do not allow other people to get in the way of their goal accomplishments. Obviously, with this type of approach, high achievers do not always get along well with other people.

Also, high achievers are likely to enjoy jobs with pay incentives that are clearly linked to performance and situations in which managers set challenging goals that, when reached result in tangible rewards.

The Affiliation Motive

Affiliation may be defined as "the degree to which people seek approval from others, confirm to their wishes and avoid conflicts or confrontations with others". Those with high needs for affiliation express the greatest desire to be socially accepted by others.

The study of affiliation is further complicated by the view that some behavioral scientists hold that it is an unlearned motive. Going as far back the Hawthorne Studies, the importance of the affiliation motive in the behavior of organizational participants has been very clear. Employees, especially rank-and-file employees, have a very intense need to belong to and be accepted by the group.

The Security Motive

On the surface, security appears to be much simpler than other secondary motives, for it is based largely on fear and is avoidance oriented. Very briefly, it can be said that people have a learned security motive to protect themselves from the contingencies of life and actively try to avoid situations that would prevent them from satisfying their primary, general and secondary motives.

In reality, security is much more complex than it appears on the surface. There is the simple, conscious security motive described above but there also seems to be another type of security motive that is much more complicated and difficult to identify. This latter form of security is largely unconscious but may greatly influence the behavior of many people. The simple, conscious security motive is typically taken care of by insurance programs, personal savings plans and other benefits at the place of employment.

As all other professions, a teacher would also like to have job security. Although government colleges provide security of job, still jobs with private colleges are far from secure. Further the government drive to kind of ban recruitment of new teachers, has given way to a new type of employment of teachers i.e. of "clock hour basis" or what they normally are called "visiting faculties". One may find many youngsters as being employed on this system which offers little job security. They keep hopping from one institute to the other institute in search earning more for their livelihood. The money in return what they get is also very meager. Seeing this picture one of the next generation i.e. the present student would hardly dream of coming in this profession.

The Status Motive

Although the symbols of status are considered a unique by-product of modern society like car, clothes, telecommunication equipments. The fact is that status has been in existence since there have been two or more persons on the earth.

Status can be simply defined as "the relative ranking that a person holds in a group, organization or society". Under this definition any time two or more persons are together a status hierarchy will evolve, even if both seem to have equal attributes. The symbols of status attempt to represent only the relative ranking of the person in the status hierarchy. The definition also corrects the common misconception that status means "high status." Everyone has status, but it may be high or low, depending on how the relative positions are ranked.

Status-determining factors generally have quite different meanings, depending on the values of the particular culture. An example of the impact of cultural values on status is the personal qualities of people. In some cultures, the older people are the higher their status. However, in other cultures, once a person reaches a certain age, the status goes downhill. It must be remembered that such cultural values are highly volatile and change with the times and circumstances.

Teachers earlier enjoyed very high-status in the society. So they didn't mind even working on meager salaries. However times have changed. Teachers have lost their earlier status plus their low salaries made them feel even inferior compared to other professions. Fortunately due to Six Pay Commission the salaries of teachers have gone up considerably, making surely to believe at least remuneration aspect of teaching profession has got rectified.

Intrinsic Versus Extrinsic Motives

Extrinsic motives are tangible and visible to others. They are distributed by other people (or agents). In the workplace, extrinsic motivators include pay, benefits and promotions. Extrinsic motives also include the drive to avoid punishment, such as termination or being transferred. Further, extrinsic rewards are usually contingency based. That is the extrinsic motivator is contingent on improved performance or performance that is superior to others in the same workplace. Extrinsic motivators are necessary to attract people into the organization and to keep them to the job. They are also often used to inspire workers to achieve at higher levels or to reach new goals as additional payoffs are contingent on improved performance. They do not, however, explain every motivated effort made by an individual employee.

Intrinsic motives are internally generated. In other words, they are motivators that the person associates with the task or job itself. Intrinsic rewards include feelings of responsibility, achievement, accomplishment that something was learned from an experience, feelings of being challenged or competitive or that something was an engaging task or goal. Performing meaningful work has long been associated with intrinsic motivation.

It is important to remember that these two types of motivators are not complete distinct from one another. Many motivators have both intrinsic and extrinsic components. For example, a person who wins a sales contest receives the prize, which is the extrinsic motivator. At the same time, however, "winning" in a competitive situation may be the more powerful, yet internalized, motive.

For teachers too in earlier times what mattered was the intrinsic or inner satisfaction what they were getting from doing a very pious job of passing on knowledge. However what one would observe now, it is the extrinsic motivators those are playing more important role for teachers. One would find them earning more and more money even at the cost of sacrificing some of the professional ethics.

WORK-MOTIVATION APPROACHES

The following figure graphically summarizes the various theoretical for work motivation. In particular, the figure shows three major approaches. The content theories go as far back as the turn of the 20ᵗʰ century, when pioneering scientific managers such as Frederick W. Taylor, Frank Gilbreth and Henry L. Grantt proposed sophisticated wage incentive models to motivate workers. Next came the human relations movement and then the content theories of Maslow, Herzberg and Alderfer. Following the content movement were the process theories. Based mainly on the cognitive concept of expectancy, the process theories are most closely associated with the work of Victor Vroom, Lyman Porter and Ed Lawler. More recently, equity and its derivative procedural/ organizational justice theories have received the most attention in work motivation.

At present there is a lack of integration or synthesis of the various theories. In addition to the need for integration, a comprehensive assessment of the status of work-motivation theory also noted the need for contingency models and group/ social processes. At present the content and process theories have become explanations for work motivation and there is continued research interest in equity and organization justice theories but also no agreed-upon overall theory exists.

Unlike most of the constructs in organizational behavior review conclude that there has been relatively little new theory-building and research in work motivation in recent years. As Steers concluded, "over the past decade little will be found focusing on genuine theoretical development in this area."

Theories of Motivation

All the theories can be classified into two broad categories-early theories and contemporary theories. Early theories include Scientific Management and Human Relations Model. Contemporary theories are further classified into (a) Content, (b) Process and (c) Reinforcement categories.

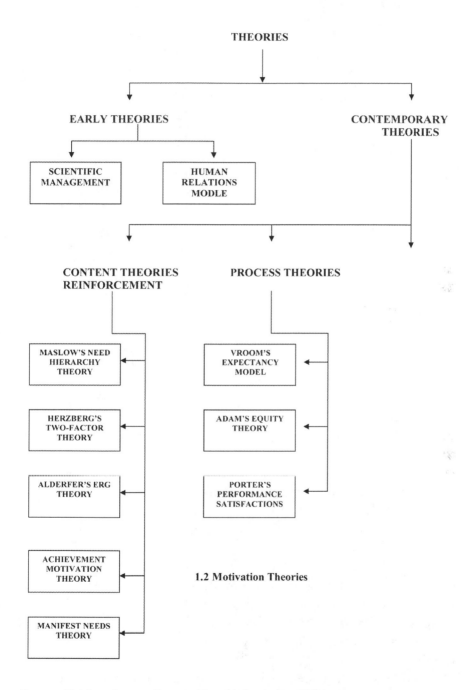

(Source: K.Ashwathappa, Organizational behavior, p. 194)

2 EARLY THEORIES

Scientific Management

Several luminaries contributed their ideas to the philosophy of Scientific Management but the movement is more associated with F.W. Taylor who is remembered as the "Father of Scientific Management". Scientific Management had contributed several techniques which are related even today. The techniques are:

- Scientific method of doing work, planning the task, scientific selection, training and remuneration of workers, standardization, specialization and division of work, time and motion studies, mental revolution.

Coupled with Taylor's logical and rational approach to management was simple theory of human behavior. People are primarily motivated by economic rewards and will take direction if offered an opportunity to improve their economic positions. Put simply, Taylor's theory stated that: Physical work could be scientifically studied to determine the optimal method of performing a job.

1. Workers could thereafter be made more efficient by being given prescriptions for how they were to do their jobs.
2. Workers would be willing to adhere to these prescriptions if paid on a differential piece work basis.

Taylor was a brilliant engineer and with his sheer observing nature he could travel from the post of a normal worker to the engineer within the time of six years. His work like finding out one best way of doing work in scientific way, scientific selection and training of workers are worth admiring.

However what Taylor has been criticized heavily by behavioral scientists is that he treated worker or man as just another factor of production like machines. He thought workers could be motivated by offering them more and more money as incentive for their better performance where it was proved by behavioral scientists that more than money, it's the working environment, group pressures, interpersonal relations play more role in motivating people. Further Taylor's concept of division of labour which resulted into repetitive & boring tasks themselves are also considered to be one of the demotivating factors.

However contribution of Taylor is being appreciated even now as well as when he was alive. For example, according to Peter Druker, Taylor's work has had the same degree of impact upon the world as the work of Karl Marx or Sigmund Freud.

Human Relations Model

Eventually, it became clear that the assumption that workers were primarily motivated by money, proved to be inadequate. Elton Mayo and other human relations researchers found that the social contacts which the workers had at work places were also important and that the boredom and repetitiveness of tasks were themselves factors in reducing motivation. Mayo and others also believed that managers could motivate employees by acknowledging their social needs and by making workers feel useful and important.

As a result, employees were given some freedom to make their own decisions on their jobs. Greater attention was paid to organization's informal work groups. More information was provided to employees about the manager's intentions and about the operations of the organization.

In the scientific management model, workers had been expected to accept management's authority in return for high wages made possible by the efficient system designed by management and implemented by the workers. In the human relations model, workers were expected to accept management's authority because supervisors treated them with consideration and were attentive to their needs. The problem with the human relations model is its undue reliance on social contacts at work situation for motivating employees. Social contacts, though desirable by themselves will not always help to motivate workers.

The findings of Elton Mayo are considered very important for field of organizational behaviour where he proved that the organization is a social system and the human relations at the work place decide the equations of performance of workers. Although human relation is not only one variable which decides the performance; still it plays a significant role. Mayo's work is considered to be the very foundation for the field of organization behaviour where the concept of man as an "Economic Model" who can be motivated by economic rewards was rejected and more research was started on the worker's psychology at the work place.

3 CONTENT THEORIES

Maslow's Need Hierarchy Theory, Herzberg's Two-Factor Theory, Alderfer's ERG Theory, McClelland's Achievement Theory and Murray's Manifest Needs theories are classified as content theories. These theories use individual needs to help in the understanding of job satisfaction and work behaviors.

Stated more clearly, content theorists suggest that the manager's job is to create work environment that respond positively to individual needs. Such things as poor performance, undesirable behaviors and decreased satisfactions can be partially explained in terms of dissatisfied needs. Also, the motivational value and rewards can be analeyed in terms of "activated" needs to which a given reward either does or does not respond.

Maslow's Need Hierarchy Theory

The Need Hierarchy Model of motivation propounded by Abraham Harold Maslow is undoubtedly the simplest and most widely discussed theory of motivation. The essence of the theory may be summarized thus:

1. People are wanting beings whose needs can influence their behavior. Only unsatisfied needs can influence behavior, satisfied need do not act as motivators.
2. Needs are many, so they are arranged in an order of importance or hierarchy, from the basic to the complex.

3. The person advances to the next level of hierarchy or from the basic to the complex, only when the lower level need is at least minimally satisfied.

4. Further up the hierarchy the person is able to go, the more individuality, humanness and psychological health he will display.

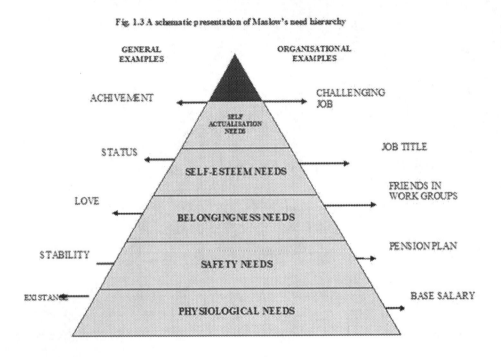

Fig. 1.3 A schematic presentation of Maslow's need hierarchy

(Source: K.Ashwathappa, Organizational behavior, p. 196)

The Needs:

The most basic level of needs comprises the primary or physiological ones. So long as they are unsatisfied, they monopolies a person's consciousness and have virtually exclusive power to motivate behavior. However, when they are satisfied, they cease to be motivators.

The satisfaction of primary needs does not produce contentment; instead of it unleashes a new series of discontents. The secondary needs now begin to acquire the power to motivate. People do not stop wanting; after physiological needs are fulfilled. They begin to want, in succession, safety, love, esteem and self-realization. Maslow also suggested that people can travel down as well as up the hierarchy. Loss of existing satisfaction of primary needs, for example, can reactivate that level and increase its relative importance. A detailed description of each level needs follows.

Physiological Needs:

The most basic, powerful and obvious of all human needs is the need for physical survival. Included in this group are the needs for food, drink, oxygen, sleep, sex, protection from extreme and sensory stimulation. These physiological drives are directly concerned with the biological maintenance of the organism and motivated by higher order needs.

The chronically hungry person will never strive to compose music or build a brave new world. Such a person is much too preoccupied with getting something to eat. In the organizational context, physiological needs are represented by employees concern for salary and basic working conditions. It is the duty of managers to ensure that these needs of the employees are met so that they can be motivated to strive for gratification of higher order needs.

Safety Needs:

The primary motivating force here is to ensure a reasonable degree of continuity, order, structure and predictability in one's environments. Maslow suggested that the safety needs are most readily observed in infants and young children because of their relative helplessness and dependence on adults.

Safety needs exert influence beyond childhood. The preference for secured income, the acquisition of insurance and owning one's own house may be regarded as motivated in part by safety motive. At least in part, religious and philosophic belief systems may also be interpreted in this fashion.

Security needs in the organizational context correlate to such factors as job security, salary increases, safe working conditions, unionization and lobbying for protective legislation. Managerial practices to satisfy the safety needs of employees include pension scheme, group insurance, provident fund, gratuity, safe working conditions, grievance procedure, system of seniority to govern lay-off and others. Arbitrary or unpredictable actions, actions which create feeling of uncertainty (particularly regarding continued employment), favoritism or discrimination on the part of superiors hardly create feeling of security in an employee's mind.

Belonging and Love Needs:

These needs arise when physiological and safety needs are satisfied. An individual motivated on this level for affectionate relationship with others, namely, for a place in his or her family and/or reference groups. Group membership becomes a dominant goal for the individual. Accordingly, the person will feel keenly the pains of loneliness, social ostracism, friendlessness and rejection, especially when induced by the absence of friends, relatives a spouse or children.

Unlike Freud who equated love with sex, Maslow believed that love involves a healthy, loving relationship between two people, which include mutual respect, admiration and trust. Maslow also stressed that love needs involve both giving and receiving love.

In the organizational context, social needs represent the need for a compatible work group, peer acceptance, professional friendship and friendly supervision. Managers do well when they encourage informal groups. Besides, supervision needs to be effective and friendly.

Unfortunately, many managers view friendly relations of employees with their peers as a treat to the organization and act accordingly. Managers have often gone to considerable lengths to control and direct employees relationships in ways that are opposed to the natural grouping of human beings. Therefore when a manager assumes that informal groups threaten the organization and actively strives to break up existing groups, the individuals affected may become resistant, antagonistic and uncooperative. These resistant actions are often consequences or symptoms, not causes. The manager may have actually thwarted the satisfaction of social needs and perhaps even safety needs.

Self-Esteem Needs:

Next in Maslow's hierarchy are esteem or egoistic needs. Maslow classified these needs into two subsidiary sets: self-respect and esteem from others. The former includes such things as desire for competence, confidence, personal strength, adequacy, achievement, independence and freedom. An individual needs to know that he is worthwhile and capable of mastering tasks and challenges in life. Esteem from others includes prestige, recognition, acceptance, attention, status, reputation and appreciation. In this case individual needs to be appreciated for what they can do, i.e. they must experience feelings of worth because their competence is recognized and valued by others.

Satisfaction of the self-esteem needs generates feelings and attitudes of self-confidence, worth, strength, capability and of being useful and necessary in the world. In contrast, the thwarting of these needs, leads to feelings and attitudes of inferiority, ineptness, weakness and helplessness. These negative self-perceptions, may in turn give rise to basic discouragement, sense of futility and hopelessness in dealing with life's demands and a low evaluation of self vis-a-vis others. Maslow emphasized that the healthiest self-esteem is based on earned respect from others rather on fame, status or adulation. Esteem is the result of effort—it is earned. Hence, there is a real psychological danger of basing one's esteem needs on the opinions of others rather than on real ability, achievement and adequacy. Once a person relies exclusively upon the opinions of others for his own self-esteem, he places himself in psychological jeopardy. To be solid, self-esteem must be founded on one's actual worth rather than on external factors beyond one's control.

On the work place self-esteem needs correspond to job title, merit pay increase, peer/ supervisory recognition, challenging work, responsibility and publicity in company publications. Managerial practices to fulfill these needs include challenging work assignments, performance feedback, performance recognition, personal encouragement and involving employees in goal getting and decision-making.

Self-Actualization Needs:

Finally, if all the earlier four level needs are satisfied, the need for self-actualization comes to the fore. Maslow characterized self-actualization as the desire to become everything that one is capable of becoming. The person who has achieved this highest level presses towards the full use and exploitation of his talents, capacities and potentialities. In other words, to self-actualize is to become the total kind of person that one wants to become to reach the peak of one's potential.

The need for self-actualization is distinctive, in that it is never fully satisfied. It appears to remain important and insatiable. The more apparent satisfaction of it a person obtains, the more important the need for more seems to become.

Though the impulse to realize one's potential is natural and necessary, only a few, usually the gifted, ever do so. Maslow himself estimated that less than one per cent of the population fulfills the need for self-actualization. Maslow advances three reasons for this. First, people are invariably blind to their own potentialities. Second the social environment often stifles development towards self-fulfillment. Women, for example were stereotyped for long to be housewives. This prevented them from reaching self-fulfillment. A final obstacle is the strong negative influence exercised by the safety needs. The growth process demands a constant willingness to take risks, to make mistakes and to break old habits. This requires courage. It logically follows that anything that increases the individual's fear and anxiety also increases his tendency to regress towards safety and security.

In an organization, self-actualization needs correlate to desire for excelling oneself in one's job, advancing an important idea, successfully managing a unit and the like. By being aware of the self-actualization needs of subordinates, managers can use a variety approaches to enable subordinates to achieve personal as well as organizational goals.

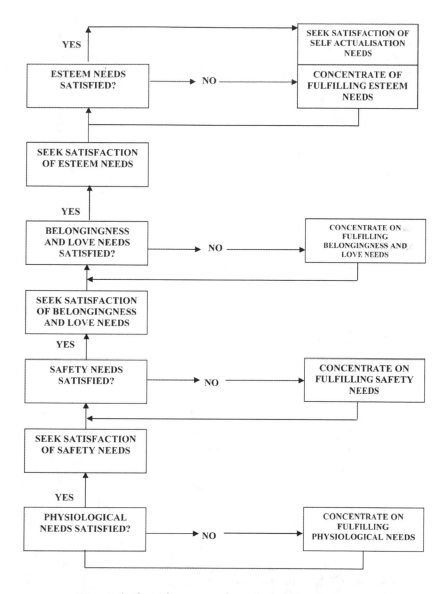

Fig. 1.4 Flow diagram of needs satisfaction

(Source: T.Herbert, Dimensions of Organizational Behaviour, p. 23)

Deficit Motivation versus Growth Motivation

In addition to his hierarchical conception of motivation, Maslow distinguished two broad categories of human motives: deficit motives and growth motives. The former (also designated as deficiency or D motives by Maslow) reflect little more than the lower needs in Maslow's motivation hierarchy, especially those concerned with the organism's physiological and safety requirements. The aim of deprivation motivation is to fend off organism tension arising through deficit states, e.g. a hunger, cold. In this sense, D motives are urgent determinants of behavior.

In contrast to D-type motives, growth motives (also designated as meta needs or B motives) are distinct goals associated with the inborn urge to actualize one's inherent potentials. The objective of growth motives or meta needs is to enrich living by enlarging experiences, thus increasing the joy of being alive. Growth motivation does not involve the repairing of deficit states (i.e. tension reduction) as much as the expansion of horizons (i.e. tension increase).

Theory at a glance:

According to Maslow there are five levels of needs viz Physiological needs, safety security, love and belongingness, self esteem and self actualization. A human being firstly tries to satisfy lower order needs. Satisfaction of lower order need gives rise to inducement for satisfaction of higher order needs. Maslow has proposed the sequence of needs according to the priority of needs in the lives of human beings. According to Maslow at a time, only one need operates. A satisfied need stops giving motivation to the individual. Then the individual moves to the satisfaction of higher order need.

Evaluation of Need Hierarchy Model

Maslow's need hierarchy theory has been highly appreciated. It is considered to be the fundamental theory of motivation. It is helpful for managers to understand different needs of employees and treat them accordingly. Maslow's theory has pointed out different needs of human beings.

Secondly many times managers seem to be puzzled what is the reason that money seems to be a motivating factor in case of one employee but completely not helpful for motivating the other employee. Manager may also puzzle how in the same working environment, one employee is working with motivation where the other is loafing around. The theory gives answers to such questions that they are on different levels of hierarchy of needs.

Third, the theory also points out the human beings are not stagnant as far as needs are concerned. They continuously strive to satisfy their present needs. The process does not end as the satisfaction of one need gives birth to another need and again human being will strive to achieve another level of need. The theory shows the dynamism of needs.

Fourth, Maslow's approach to human behavior marks a total departure from earlier approaches. He pointed out humanistic psychology, based on existential philosophy. According to the theory, a man is a healthy, good and creative being, capable of carving out his own destiny. The philosophy prompted Maslow to conceptualize self-actualization needs whereby man tries to achieve his full potential. One may argue with this very concept but, the work of Maslow must be appreciated because of his departure from Freud who was obsessed with sex and Skinner who sought to extend observations derived from animal research to human behavior.

Finally, the theory deserves appreciation for its simplicity, commonness, humanness and intuitiveness.

However, Need Hierarchy Theory has been criticized by many and the number of critics exceeds the number who supports the theory.

First, it is criticized that Maslow's theory is not the theory of motivation at work place. Malsow himself did not intend to carve out the theory for organizational situational until 20 years after he proposed the theory. Despite this lack of intent on Maslow's part, others, such as Douglas McGregor, in his widely read book "The Human Side of Enterprise", popularized Maslow's theory in management literature.

Second, many would argue the hierarchy of needs just simply doesn't exist. All needs are operative simultaneously. A person striving to satisfy love and belongingness need just can't afford to forget physiological need of food.

Thirdly there is no particular sequence of needs for individuals. For some people, the need of self-actualization can be more important to be achieved and they are not bothered about physiological needs. The example of it can be Indian Hrishis and Munis (Saints and Sages) who would involve themselves in spiritualism, meditation; being completely away from the world for the ultimate goal of "Moksha" without being bothered about even basic need of shelter or food. So person may jump to the upper hierarchy of needs skipping the lower order needs

Fourth, not only are there differences across countries in needs hierarchy, there are variations within countries and among individuals. Within a country, culturally disadvantaged employees may feel stronger deprivation of lower level needs, whereas culturally advantaged employees seek satisfaction of higher level needs. The evidence of it can be found in the Indian Caste system or in USA with white majority and black minority whereby the needs of socially backward communities are found to be different than that of the socially advantaged groups.

Fifth, Maslow's assumption after satisfaction of lower order needs, person moves to the next higher level of needs seem to be challenged. Some individuals may remain satisfied with lower order need of safety and security and may not move upward on the hierarchy of needs.

Sixthly, neither managers have time to diagnose each employees need and its level nor the reward packages can be tailored to the needs of each individual employee.

Lastly, Maslow's theory is culture bound crafted out considering western culture. Maslow says behind every action of employee, there is a purpose or expectation of reward which may not come true in case of eastern culture like that of India wherein its spiritual scripture Bhagwadgeeta says that "Just do your work, don't expect rewards" (Karmanye wa dhikaraste ma faleshu kadachan)

In spite of its serious limitations, Need Hierarchy Theory is important because this is an attempt to find out different types of human needs. In an organization, it can certainly be helpful for managers to understand the fundamental fact that different workers have got different needs. Especially needs of esteem and self actualization are very important from the perspective of organizational performance.

Application of the theory to the Teaching Profession:

As originally the Need Hierarchy Theory was not made for organizational motivation, but to find out general human needs, it is also applicable to teachers being human beings. All the levels of needs apply to teaching profession. The only difference is that their application of sequence seems to have changed over a period of time.

In earlier times, the need of esteem or status was found to be very prominent among teachers to an extent that there was less concern for physiological needs like money or monetary rewards. Teachers enjoyed a very high esteem in the society. One could particularly find this true in case of the old Indian Education system of 'Gurukul' where a teacher or guru was happy passing on knowledge to his disciples at almost no cost and being least bothered about materialistic gains. In fact the Guru would be the one who would provide food and shelter to his disciples. Passing on knowledge was considered to be a pious work, for not being equated to any monetary gains.

Some of the famous Indian intellectuals who later turned into teachers like Gurudeb Rabindranath Tagore could reach to self-actualization level but never seem to have cared for monetary gains. Refusing to accept title "Sir" from the Queen of England goes on to show his idea of esteem was not dependent on opinion or titles from others but it was based on his real abilities, his actual worth.

However times have changed. Neither the self-esteem nor the self-actualization seems to matter for teachers. They have gone back to the lower order needs especially money. Money has become a matter of concern where teachers are ready to change their institutional loyalties, moving to other organization which offers more pay. With such mobility there is little concern or love and belongingness for the organization or for students. They are ready to sacrifice security of job in a college and work for a private coaching institution simply because it offers them more money with the least of efforts. One can't generalize this in case of all teachers. There are still those dedicated and committed teachers; only matter of concern is that their number is dwindling with times. In case of these teachers, self-esteem needs are found to be very strong. Such a teacher may leave a high salaried job for the sake of dignity and work on low salaried job. As it has been criticized at the onset itself, Malsow's theory of motivation is not the theory of work motivation but has categorized human needs into general five categories; so it does apply to teaching profession too but only in marginal sense.

McGregor's Participation Model Theory:

Douglous McGregor put forward in his book "Human Side of Enterprise" two sets of assumptions about human beings which he thought were implied by the actions of autocratic and permissive managers. The first set of assumptions is contained in "Theory X" and the second set of assumptions in "Theory Y". It is important to note that these assumptions were not based on any research, but are intuitive deductions.

Theory X

'Theory X' believes that autocratic managers often make the following assumptions about their subordinates. Accordingly, the subordinate in general:

- Has an inherent dislike for work and will avoid it, if he can.
- Is lazy and avoids responsibility and power.
- Is indifferent to organizational goals.
- Prefers to be directed, wishes to avoid responsibility, has relatively little ambition and wants security above all.

According to McGregor, this is a traditional theory of what workers like and what management must do to motivate them. Workers have to persuaded and pushed into performance. This is management's task. Management can offer rewards to a worker who shows higher productivity and can punish him if his performance is below standard. This is also called "carrot and stick" approach to motivation. It suggests that threats of punishment and strict control are the ways to control the people. McGregor questioned the assumptions of Theory X which followed "carrot and stick" approach to motivation of people and suggested autocratic style of leadership. He felt that management by direction and control is a questionable method for motivating such people whose physiological and safety needs have been satisfied and whose social, esteem and self-actualization needs are becoming important. For such people, Theory Y seems to be applicable.

Theory Y assumes that the goals of the organization and those of the individuals are not necessarily incongruent. The basic problem in most of the organizations is that of securing commitment of the workers to organizational goals. Worker's commitment is directly related to the satisfaction of their needs. Inspite of development in education, science and technology, many industrial houses and public sectors in India function under traditional and negative attitudes as mentioned above. They make use of Theory X principles to get the work done. McGregor's theory places great emphasis on satisfaction of the needs, particularly higher ones, of the employees. It does not rely heavily on the use of authority as an instrument of command and control. It assumes that employees excise self-direction and self-control in the direction of the goals to which they feel themselves committed. They could be motivated by delegation of authority, job enlargement, management by objectives and participative management practices. Theory Y is not useful for all sort of industrial undertakings. Theory X is effective for less developed and underdeveloped workers. Theory Y is feasible only for developed and educated workers who are responsible and ambitious.

Theory Y

Managers with 'Theory Y' orientation make the following assumptions about their subordinates. Accordingly, subordinates in general:

- Does not inherently dislike work. Depending upon controllable conditions, work may be a source of satisfaction or a source of punishment.
- Will exercise self-direction and self-control in the service of objectives to which he is committed.
- Commitment to objectives is a function of the rewards associated with their achievement.
- Learns under proper conditions, not only to accept, but also to seek responsibility.
- The capacity to exercise a relatively high degree of imagination, ingenuity and creativity in the solution of organizational problems is widely, not narrowly, distributed in the population.

Japanese Management

Japanese management can be characterized by the following principles: (a) an emphasis on the group rather than the individual; (b) an emphasis on human rather than functional relationships and (c) a view of top management as generalists and facilitators rather than as decision-makers.

Theory Z

Tremendous international attention is now being focused on the outstanding performance of the Japanese economy and style of management and the success of management practices being adopted by various Japanese firms. Interest in Japanese management has rapidly increased in America and other countries. William Ouchi made a comparison of America and Japanese management practices and concluded that many of the Japanese management practices can be adopted in American context. He suggested the adoption of Theory Z. It may be noted that Theory Z is not a theory in the true sense. It is merely a label interchangeable with type Z. It describes human behaviour as in the case of theories X and Y. The expression 'Theory Z' was adopted not for analytical purpose but for promotional purpose. It may be noted that the label Z has been used by Urwick, Rangnekar and Ouchi. But Ouchi's views have got much publicity.

Key Elements of Theory Z
- Strong bond between the company and the Employees.
- Group Participation.
- Mutual Trust.
- Non Hierarchical Organizational Structure.
- Human Resource Development.

Theory at a Glance

Douglous McGregor's Theory X and Theory Y is based on the assumptions about how management treats its employees. Theory X has total negative view about employees and it assumes that people have inherent dislike for work and they must be coerced in a way to get the work done through employees. It proposes carrot and stick approach i.e. rewards for good performance and punishment for mistakes. It assumes that employees need to be directed and controlled.

On the other hand, Theory Y is based on positive assumptions about employees. It says employees like the work just the way they would like to play or relax. Employees not only accept responsibilities but in given an appropriate environment seek new responsibilities. They are self directed and controlled. So there is no need on the part of management to direct or control them. According to the theory, the abilities of problem solving and decision making are widely distributed among employees.

Theory K

American gave theory X and theory Y, which reflect the cultural element of extreme individualism. Japanese evolved theory Z which reflects the cultural element of small group cohesion and the team spirit. The Indian ideal type theory is theory K i.e. theory 'Kutumbh' the members of the organization are viewed as part of the 'kutumbh'; new people management (NPM) aims at harmonic organization practicing value based holistic management. Theory K, views all employees as part of the Kutumbh rather than resources to be manipulated by the management as is usually assumed in most modern management theories. In this approach, people do not fear the chief executives rather, have an open access to him without any fear. Chief executives and the members of the top management team set up high moral values. Intrinsic reward is welcome. Extrinsic reward is fair and open in addition to inner compensations. Chief executive is an upkeeper of organizational morality and employees feel energized in the presence of such a leader. Hence, management practices based on this theory can make the organizations more humanistic and harmonic. As the theory is based on the idea, Employee Sukhe Suktam Santha and is rooted in the Indian mode of thinking; it may provide greater insights in understanding the organizational processes. Theory 'K' is an ideal type of concept, it tends to make the organization more humanistic, more value base and more holistic.

However McGregor says that both the theories are applicable in a particular type of situation. They can't be applied to all the workers. The employees whose lower order needs i.e. physiological and safety needs are not satisfied or whose skills are not developed or are underdeveloped, Theory X is more appropriate and in case of mature, developed and educated workers, Theory Y suits more. So the application of both the theories depends upon the type of workers, a manager gets to handle.

In recent times there has been a talk of Theory Z which is based on Japanese principles of Management of Group work rather than individual work, affiliation to the organization and mutual trust between management and employees.

Theory K is based on Indian ethos which considers an organization as 'kutumbh' i.e. a family and its employees as family members. The CEO acts friend, philosopher and guide for the members. This theory is little heard of. Even Indian organizations are nowadays run on American style of Theories more and more. There are definitely some exceptions like organizations TATA or Infosys. But the number can be counted on fingers. Few CEOs like Narayan Murthy and Ratan Tata can serve as role models for their employees.

Application of the theory to the Teaching Profession:

In case of teaching profession, the environment in which a teacher works can be said to be influenced by Theory X. As it is said environment in Indian universities, is punishment-oriented. A Nobel Prize winning teacher may fail to get a ten rupee raise in his salary because no rules exist about it but he could be suspended or penalized on flimsy administrative lapses or for minor economic irregularities. He might become an easy victim of his colleagues' conspiracy who in academic areas may not come to his knees.

If we try to find the answer to the problem of poor performance of Indian academic institutions the reason is centralized system of funding and excessive bueaucratic controls which distrusts teacher at every level. For attending a conference abroad on his own expenses, a teacher has to go through several hurdles of formalities; one can understand what must be the condition if he is asking for financial assistance for attending the same conference. We find Theory X in operation as far as treatment of teacher is concerned

On the other hand, experiments of application of Theory Y to the teaching profession have failed. University and college teachers are given autonomy with an assumption that they will try to maintain all possible high standards of performance and also will fight against all those who are trying to lower down the standards. The concept of autonomy is accepted in words only; but not in spirit. One can hardly find teachers taking classes regularly and also making up for the missed classes on account of genuine reason. Teachers lack accountability. They are not accountable to the management. They don't like to be evaluated by management, peers or teachers or even by themselves. Theory Y calls for self-direction and self-control. This element seems to be completely missing in case of teachers. As far as Theory K application is concerned, it says the head of the institution serve as a role model and set up high moral values. Wherein in teaching people holding post like VC are accused of using all immoral approaches for reaching to the post. They do serve as role models whereby other teachers too resort to unethical practices. The atmosphere of family can be hardly found in Indian education institutions where careerism, competition is so rampant, people won't hesitate climbing up career ladder lynching others coming in the way.

So is the application of Theory X right to the teaching profession? Then what about those dedicated teachers who require autonomy and lack of which make them go abroad for being part of the same profession? Theory X will kill the ingenuity and creativity from among the committed teachers.

Definitely Theory Y is the solution to the problem. Teaching is a kind of profession where a teacher must be self directed and self controlled and accountable to himself first for his duties. A genuine teacher needs and likes autonomy for applying creativity. Any kind of coercion will not result in positive results. The crux of the problem is recruiting those candidates who have genuine love for teaching profession. There is no need for such teachers of any kind of control. Autonomy is the answer. But as the Theory Y too is situational it is applicable to genuine, dedicated, committed teachers. Same can be said about Theory Z.

Motivation—Hygiene Theory

Another very popular theory of motivation is that proposed by psychological Frederick Herzberg. This model, which is also termed the

Two-Factor, the Dual Factor Theory and the Motivation-Hygiene Theory has been widely accepted by managers concerned with the problem of human behavior at work.

There are two distinct aspects of the Motivation-Hygiene theory. The first and more basic part of model represents a formally stated theory of work behavior. The second aspect of Herzberg's work has focused upon the behavioral consequences of job enrichment and job satisfaction programs.

Herzberg and his associates Mausner, Peterson and Capwell began their initial work on factors affecting work motivation in the mid-50s. Their first effort entailed a thorough review of existing research to the date on the subject. Based on this review, Herzberg carried out his now famous survey of 200 accountants and engineers. Herzberg used the Critical Incident Method of obtaining data for analysis. The respondents essentially asked two questions: (1) When did you feel particularly good about your job? and (2) When did you feel exceptionally bad about your job?

The responses obtained from the Critical Incident Method were interesting. It was revealed that factors which made respondents feel good were totally different from those which made them feed bad. As seen in Fig. 1.5 certain characteristics tend to be consistently related to job-satisfaction (factors on the right-side of the figure) and others to job-dissatisfaction (factors on the left-side of the figure).

Intrinsic factors, such as achievement, recognition, the work itself, responsibility, advancement and growth seem to be related to job-satisfaction. These factors are variously known as motivators, satisfiers and job content factors. When questioned when they felt good about their work, respondents tended to attribute these characteristics to themselves. On the other hand, when they were dissatisfied, they tended to extrinsic factors, such as company policy and administration, supervision, work conditions, salary, status, security and interpersonal relations. These factors are also known as dissatisfiers, hygiene factors, maintenance factors or job context factors.

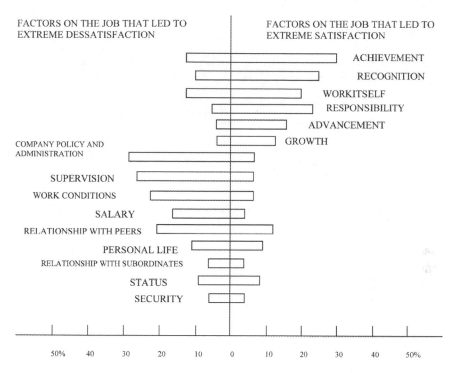

FACTORS ON THE JOB THAT LED TO
EXTREME DESSATISFACTION

FACTORS ON THE JOB THAT LED TO
EXTREME SATISFACTION

ACHIEVEMENT
RECOGNITION
WORKITSELF
RESPONSIBILITY
ADVANCEMENT
GROWTH
COMPANY POLICY AND
ADMINISTRATION
SUPERVISION
WORK CONDITIONS
SALARY
RELATIONSHIP WITH PEERS
PERSONAL LIFE
RELATIONSHIP WITH SUBORDINATES
STATUS
SECURITY

50%   40   30   20   10   0   10   20   30   40   50%

Fig. 1.5 Satisfiers and Dissatisfiers compared

(Source: K.Ashwathappa, Organizational behavior, p. 207)

According to Herzberg, satisfaction and dissatisfaction are not opposite poles of one dimension, they are two separate dimensions. Satisfaction is affected by motivators and dissatisfaction is caused by hygiene factors. This is the key idea of Herzberg and it has important implications for managers.

To achieve motivation, managers should cope with both, satisfiers and dissatisfiers. Improvement in hygiene factors results in removal of dissatisfaction from the minds of employees. A favorable frame of mind is now created for motivation. Provide satisfiers, motivation will then take place. Managers should be realistic not to expect motivation by only improving the "hygienic" work environment.

This is the crux of the two-factor theory of motivation. Fig.1.6 diagrams the essence of the Herzberg's model.

Fig. 1.6 Contrasting views of satisfaction and dissatisfaction

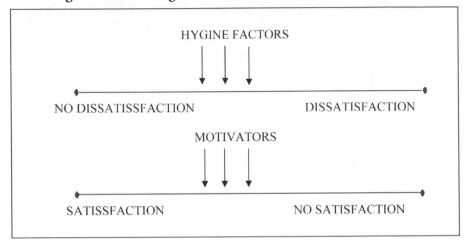

(Source: K.Ashwathappa, Organizational behavior, p. 207)

Need Hierarchy and Two-Factor Theories compared and Contrasted

There are similarities and dissimilarities between Malow's Need Hierarchy Theory and Herzberg's Hygiene-Motivation Theory. Both of them have become very popular and have been widely accepted by academics and managers. The most striking similarity between the two theories is that they assume that specific needs energize behavior. Further more, there appear to be a great deal of agreement as to the totality of human needs. Fig.1.7 shows how the needs in both the models might be related. It is reasonable to argue that Herzberg's motivators satisfy the higher order needs of Maslow's i.e. self-esteem and self-actualization.

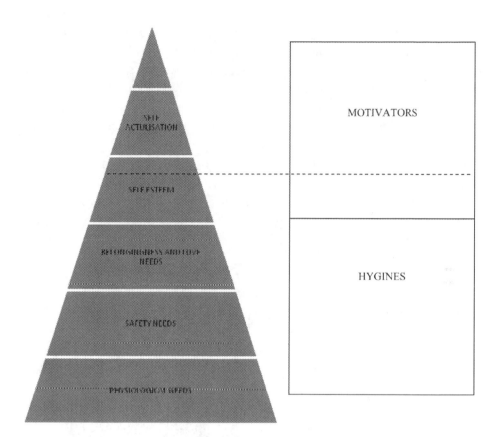

Fig. 1.7 A comparison of Maslow's need hierarchy and Herzberg's two-factor theory.

The hygiene factors are the equivalent of the physiological, security and social needs of the Need Hierarchy Model.

Theory at a glance

Unlike Maslow, Herzberg has made clear distinction between those factors that create dissatisfaction and those create satisfaction. The research was carried on using Critical Incident Method. The employees were asked basically two questions i.e. when they felt particularly good and particularly bad about the job. Based on it, he made classification of factors into hygiene and motivating factors. Hygiene factors are those whose removal creates dissatisfaction and its restoration leads to removing that dissatisfaction. However it doesn't mean the employee is now motivated. He is now neutral or one can say in a state of mind wherein he can be motivated. Hygiene factors were normally found to be related to company policy, rules, supervision, salary, job security etc. On the other hand, the motivation factors were different like responsibility, work itself, recognition, and achievement. The hygiene factors appear quite similar to the Maslow's lower hierarchy of needs whereas motivating factors appears to be quite similar to higher order of needs.

One must give credit to Herzberg for drawing attention to the fact that mere provision good salary, good working conditions or job security can not make an employee feel satisfied. Theory highlighted the fact that money can't be a motivating factor. The theory stated that managers must be more careful for motivating factors rather than concentrating on improving hygiene factors.

Evaluation of the Two-Factor Theory

All things considered, it may be stated that Herzberg's theory has been widely read and known in the fraternity of managers. There are certain merits of the theory.

1. Herzberg's work particularly is important because it stimulated lot of research work in the field of organizational motivation. The research work which was done earlier was not consistent and theory of Maslow was not even called as theory of "work motivation" but just showing the general hierarchy of human needs. That too was a clinical research or the work carried out in laboratory. Herzberg carried out his work in organization and among employees. So it is helpful in understanding work motivation.

2. Herzberg's recommendations are particularly important who brought the fact to the notice of manager that money singly can't be a factor of motivation. It is the job and its design that is more important and managers must provide attention in making job of employee as interesting as possible. For the reason Herzberg has recommended the techniques of job enrichment and job design. The increased popularity since the mid-1960 of vertically expanding jobs to allow workers greater responsibility in planning

and controlling their work can be largely attributed to Herzber's findings and recommendations.

Like the Need Hierarchy Theory, the Hygiene-Motivation Theory has been subject of appreciation and criticism. The criticisms of the theory are the following:

1. Many researchers have criticized the very classification of motivation and hygine factor. According to them the methodology applied is limited. It is found that employees are taking credit for whatever right is happening and they feel satisfied because of it and blames external factors like company policy for their dissatisfaction.

2. The reliability of the results are also challenged on the ground that it is based on lot of subjectivity i.e. interpretation made by the researchers. The same response by 2 employees can be treated differently by the researchers.

3. It is argued that the theory is basically theory of job satisfaction and not motivation. There has been no relation established between job satisfaction and productivity in the theory. Whether the job satisfaction really gets translated into higher productivity, can a satisfied employee be productive employee; the theory fails to provide answer to it.

4. The theory fails to explain the overall measure of satisfaction. There are different factors for which an employee is not happy still he feels satisfied about the job.

5. The distinction made between hygiene and motivation factor is also not applicable to all the employees. One factor that appears to be a hygiene factor for one employee may be actually a motivating factor for the other employee. Relative influence of the two factors vary according to occupational levels

6. As the research has been carried out among white collar employees, its applicability to blue collar employees is in doubt.

Application of the theory to the Teaching Profession:

The theory has great significance to the teaching profession. One certainly needs to look into the aspect of what creates dissatisfaction among teachers and what motivates them for better performance. As the original theory was carried out among white collar employees i.e. accountants and engineers, the same kind of research can be conducted to find out hygiene and motivation factors for teachers. The answer may come out different than what theory says. Both hygiene and motivating factors can vary for teaching community.

ERG Theory

The E, R and G of ERG theory stands for existence, relatedness and growth, the three sets of needs which are the focus of this alternative theory of human needs in the organizations. Existence needs, perceived as necessary for basic human existence, roughly correspond to the physiological and security needs of Maslow's hierarchy. Relatedness needs, the desire we have for maintaining interpersonal relations are similar to Maslow's belongingness and esteem needs. Finally, an intrinsic desire for personal development growth needs, are analogous to Maslow's needs for self-esteem and self-actualization. ERG theory, developed by Alderfer, argues along with Maslow, that people do have needs that those needs are arranged in a hierarchy and that needs are important determinants of human behavior. However, the ERG Theory differs from Need Hierarchy Theory in three respects.

- First, instead of five hierarchies of needs, the ERG theory hypothesizes only three.
- Second, the need hierarchy theory postulates a rigid step like progression. The ERG theory, instead, postulates that more than one need may be operative at the same time. In other words, Alderfer suggests that there does not exist a rigid hierarchy where a lower need must be substantially gratified before one can move on. A person can be working on growth even though existence or relatedness needs are unsatisfied.
- Third, Maslow argues that a person will stay at a certain level until that need is satisfied. The ERG Theory counters this by noting that when a higher level need is frustrated, the individual's desire to increase a lower-level need takes place. Inability to satisfy a need for social interaction, for instance, might increase the desire for more money or for better working conditions. Thus, the ERG

Theory contains a frustration-regression dimension. Frustration at higher level can lead to regression to a lower level need (Fig.1.8).

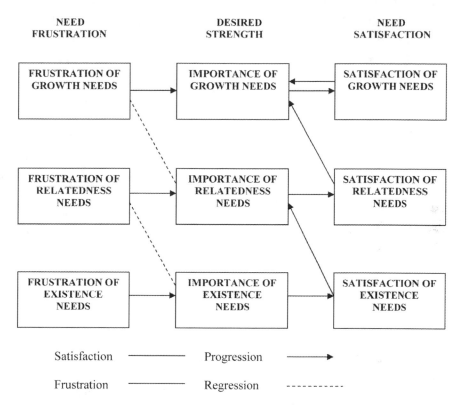

Fig. 1.8 Two Key Components of ERG Theory:
Satisfaction-Progression and Frustration-Regression

(Source: Richard M.Hodgetts, Organizational behavior, Macmillan, 1991, p.134)

Evaluation

Advantages of the ERG Theory are as follows:

1. The ERG Theory is more consistent with our knowledge of individual differences among people. Variables such as education, family background and cultural environment can alter the importance or driving force that a group of needs holds for a particular individual. The evidence demonstrates that people in

other cultures rank the need categories differently, for instance, natives of Spain and Japan place social needs before their psychological requirements. This would be consistent with the ERG theory. The ERG Theory, therefore, represents a more valid version of the need hierarchy.

2. Although there is some evidence to counter the theory's predictive value, most contemporary analysis of work motivation tends to support Alerfer's Theory over Maslow's and Herzberg's. Overall, the ERG Theory seems to take some of the strong points of the earlier content theories but is less restrictive and limiting.

Disadvantages of the theory are as follows:

The theory does not offer clear cut guidelines. The ERG Theory implies that individuals will be motivated to engage in behavior which will satisfy one of the three sets of needs postulated by the theory. In order to predict what behavior any given person will be motivated to engage in would require an assessment of that person to determine which of the three needs were most salient and most important to that person. The individuals would then be predicted to engage in behavior which would lead to the attainment of outcomes with capacity of fulfilling these salient needs.

The ERG Theory is newer than the Need Hierarchy Theory and has not yet attained such wide currency, not such a degree of research interest as has the Need Hierarchy Theory. Thus, the evidence for applicability of the ERG theory must be said to be somewhat uncertain at the moment. Alderfer's research has indicated some degree of support for the theory but in general it is simply too early to pass judgment on the overall validity of the theory.

Theory at a glance:

ERG theory stands for Existence, Relatedness and Growth. Its comparison with Maslow's Need Hierarchy Theory is inevitable. The existence need appears quite similar to Maslow's physiological and safety and security needs. The relatedness need is quite similar to love and belongingness needs of Maslow. Growth needs can be seen getting reflected in Malsow's Self-actualization and self-esteem needs. Unlike Malsow's five hierarchies of needs, there are only 3 hierarchies of needs. According to Maslow, there is a rigid sequence a human being follow for meeting 5 levels of needs. At one time, only one type of need operates and after satisfaction of that need, a human being moves to the higher order in hierarchy. But according Alderfer many needs can operate at one time. There is no rigid sequence human being follows for gratification of needs. E.g. human being may be trying to gratify his higher order of needs simultaneously trying to satisfy his existence needs. Alderfer says that if the higher order need is frustrated that may make a person e.g. try to earn more money i.e. regression to the lower order of needs.

Problem with the theory is that it says many needs operate at one time, finding out the most important need that is operating at a particular time, is important in order to motivate the person. It's a tricky thing to find out comparatively which need is more important at a given point of time. Then it can be predicted that the individual would be engaged in behavior which results in the gratification of that need. ERG Theory has not been a matter of much of the research like earlier two theories. So it deserves more research in order to pass overall judgment about the theory.

Application of the theory to Teaching Profession:

Among teachers' two set of needs appears to be very strong: Existence needs and Growth needs. Earning money in fact seems to have taken more importance which is evident in the fact the teachers are engaged in many other activities apart from their original job. Conducting coaching classes, engaging classes at other institutes, involvement in extra remunerative jobs, switching to other institute for the sake of money; organizational loyalty seem to have taken over by professional loyalty. Many of the activities for earning money can be categorized into unethical and immoral.

Aspect of 'relatedness' was very strong with teachers of earlier generations. They were closely connected to their students and did not bother about materialistic rewards in reward for their work. However the aspect of relatedness seems to be having least importance for the teachers of nowadays. Neither they have high relatedness to get attached to the students nor with the colleagues because of professional rivalry or jealousy. Only relatedness aspect can be found in formation various teachers unions which are engrossed in inter union rivalry and prime motto of fighting for more salary for teachers.

The growth need is also very strong among teachers. In case of highly committed and genuinely interested teachers, this need work in the form of publication of research work, books, getting fellowships, scholarships from prestigious institutions, winning awards; the desire appears to be very strong. However in case of those teacher who have chosen this profession as the last option and want to progress at any cost who are referred as 'teacher politicians' too, growth needs work strong. An HoD getting book written from one of his junior teachers but publishing under his name, getting elected on important committees, posts like VC using political contacts can be sited as bad examples but still they show strong growth needs operating among teachers. But still it will be appropriate to find out the influence and intensity of various needs among teachers.

Achievement Motivation Theory

Also called the Three Needs Theory, the Achievement Motivation Theory has been advocated by David C. McClelland and his associates. It was in the late 1940s that David C. McClelland and his friends began to study three needs that motivate human behavior power, affiliation and achievement. McClelland believe that each person has a need for all the three, but that people differ in the degree to which the various needs motivate their behavior.

A brief description of these three needs follows.

Need for Achievement (nAch)

Employees with a high need for achievement derive satisfaction from achieving goals. Succeeding a task is important to the high achiever. Although people with a high need for achievement are often wealthy, their wealth comes from their ability to achieve goals. In most societies goal achievement is rewarded financially. High achievers are not motivated by money per se; money is their indicator of achievement. High achievers prefer immediate feedback on their performance and they generally undertake tasks of moderate difficulty rather than those that are either every easy or very difficult. They dislike tasks with high risks because they get no achievement satisfaction from happenstance success. Similarly, they dislike easy tasks because there is no challenge to their skills. High achievers also prefer to work independently, so that successful tasks performance (or failure) can be related to their own efforts rather than to someone else's.

McClelland believes that the need for achievement can be learned and he has cited numerous instances in which people developed the need to achieve. He believes that economically backward cultures can be changed if the need to achieve can be stimulated. If McClelland is right, the achievement motivation theory is particularly attractive because the motive can be taught to an individual or a group.

That the need for achievement can be learned was demonstrated in the Kakinada project in our country, way back in 1970s. In this ambitious project, researchers attempted to raise the achievement motivation of businessmen in Kakinada. The attempt was a success. The businessmen made plans that would help them realize their goals to become successful entrepreneurs and told each other about their goals and their methods of reaching them. The businessmen became more productive as entrepreneurs; they started large industries, enlarged their business and hired more than five thousands of their villagers. In a ten year reassessment of the program, achievement motivation levels and results were still exceptional.

Developing Achievement Motives

McClelland and his associates have made specific suggestions for developing a high achievement need. They are:

1. Give employees periodic feedback on performance. This will provide information that will enable them to modify or correct their performance.
2. Provide good models of achievement. Employees who are "heroes" should be available for other to emulate.
3. Arrange tasks so that employees can pursue moderate challenges and responsibilities. Avoid tasks that are either extremely difficult or extremely easy.
4. As much as possible, employees should be able to control their own destiny and imagination. They should be trained,

however to think realistically and positively about how they will accomplish goals.

Need for Power (nPow)

The employees exhibiting the needs for power derive satisfaction from the ability to control others. Actual achievement of goals is less important than the means by which goals are achieved. Satisfaction is derived from being in positions of influence and control. Individuals with a high nPow derive satisfaction from being in positions of influence and control. Organizations that foster the power motive tend individuals with a high need for power; for example, military and political organization.

Need for Affiliation (nAff)

Individuals exhibiting this need as a dominant motive derive satisfaction from social and interpersonal activities. There is a need to form strong interpersonal ties and get close to people psychologically. If asked to choose between working at a task with those who are technically competent and those who are their friends, high nAff in individuals will choose their friends.

Evaluation the Theory

On the plus side, it may be stated that the findings of McClelland highlight the importance of bringing in line the needs of the individual and of the job. Employees with high achievement needs look for work that is challenging, satisfying, stimulating and complex. They like autonomy, variety and frequent feedback from supervisors. Employees with low achievement needs prefer situations of stability and predictability. They respond better to considerate than to impersonal high-pressure supervision and look to the work place and co-workers for social satisfaction. McClelland research also suggests that managers, to some extent, raise the achievement need level of subordinates by creating the proper work environment-permitting their subordinates a measure of independence, increasing responsibility and autonomy, gradually making tasks more challenging and praising and rewarding high performance.

Thus, McClelland's work seems to have numerous practical applications, at least in the economic realm. It would appear that the current problem is to concentrate on the development of an environment that will support the desired need, be it affiliation, power or achievement or to change the need to fit the environment.

Like any other theory on motivation, McClelland's theory too has been criticized, criticisms often being unfair. In the first place, it is questioned whether motives can be taught to adults. Considerable psychological literature suggests that the acquisition of motives normally occurs in childhood and is very difficult to change once it has been established. McClelland, however, counters that there is strong evidence from politics and religion to indicate that adult behavior can be drastically altered in a relatively short time.

The second criticism of this theory questions the contention that the needs are permanently acquired. McClelland is the only theorist who argues that the needs can be socially changed through education or training. Opponents contend that the change may be only temporary similar to the one which occurs at an evangelistic meeting or a political rally.

The third criticism relates to the methodology used by McClelland and his associates to advocate the theory. These researchers used the famous Thematic Apperception Test (TAT) of Murray as the main tool to determine basic needs. While projective techniques as TAT have many have advantages over structured questionnaires, the interpretation of responses is more subject to research's bias.

Theory at a glance

The theory suggests that there are three sets of needs, achievement, power and affiliation. According to McClelland high achievers are moderate risk takers and prefer relatively difficult task than very easy one. They want immediate feedback to their performance and would prefer to work individually in order relate their efforts to success (or failure). According to Alderfer, achievement needs can be learned or taught in adulthood too where as critics argue they can be learned only in childhood. He has given many suggestions in order to apply them in case of employees having high achievement needs like giving them immediate feedback, presenting other high achievers as role models and also adjusting work according to intensity of achievement motive. For individuals with power motive, holding a position of power or influence or control is important. Rather than achievement of the goal, the means of achieving are important for these people. The third set of needs i.e. affiliation; people get satisfaction from interpersonal or social relation. They form close interpersonal ties.

Like other theories of motivation this theory too has been criticized. The technique applied by McClelland of TAT has been criticized to be more subjective in nature. The theory suggests achievement needs can be learned even in adulthood; however critics point out they can be learned only in childhood. McClelland claims needs are permanently learned but critics argue it is only a temporary change. The good point of theory is said to be that McClelland has pointed that the job should be designed according to the needs of the employees.

Application of the theory to the Teaching Profession

Achievement Motive

Achievement motive can also be found in teachers who want to climb up on the career ladder or leave their legacy through research work or other academic achievements like scholarship or fellowship with prestigious university. There is hardly any risk associated with teaching work which a teacher would like to take. However the want of more money would make some teachers take risk on wrong things like malpractices in examinations, running private coaching classes while being employed in a college, arriving late or complete absenteeism, conducting classes in other colleges at the cost of their work in their own college. These teachers are ready to take risk as there is no strong "watch dog" or "big brother" who would observe their activities and make them pay for it. The problem with teaching community is that how to give teachers a feedback on their teaching work, who will do that and how he will do that? A proper system of teacher's performance evaluation needs to be developed where by he can know his performance. The other major problem in teaching profession is that there is no relation between performance and rewards. After a certain number of completed years of service a teacher gets automatic promotion. So there are no incentives to perform better. Until and unless a good system of evaluation or feedback is developed much of the problems concerning teacher motivation will remain unsolved. This is a real problem with teaching profession that no where rewards and performance are related which has resulted in substandard performance of teachers as there is no incentive to do well.

High achievers are not motivated by money per se. In earlier times it was true with teachers that the task of teaching itself was enough for giving teacher intrinsic or inner satisfaction. He would never care for any monetary reward. However this can't be said for today's teachers.

Preoccupations with the task, to work alone are also some of the characteristics of high achievers which can be found with highly intellectual and committed teachers although their number may be less. Some of the prestigious institutions like IITs and IIMs have been able to live up to their standard, it is because of these qualitative teachers.

Power Motive

In education field also the power motive have become dominant whereby grabbing positions of power like Vice Chancellor, Principal, Director, Head of Department, teaching fraternity seem to be ready to make all possible compromises. The selection on these posts is often made on non academic criteria and all possible influences are used for it. When highly important posts like VC or Director, principal are occupied by those who don't have any admirable academic credentials, what kind of vision they would provide to teachers, is obvious. Such people fail to create trust and also can never get respect from the teachers. Personal power is more oriented toward the ability to dominate others and to do so for the personal gain of the leader.

This is mostly used by those teacher politicians who enter the field on non academic criteria and who are least interested in teaching. They do not like those teachers who are honest in their duties and popular among students. All possible efforts are made to demotivate such good teachers.

Affiliation Motive

In earlier times teachers would have great affection for the students and the students too would respect their teachers. The teachers were ready to spend extra time for the students without charging an extra penny. In the present time however the relation between a teacher and student has become more formal and lifeless. That gets percolated into lectures which are nothing but given old age notes with dictation. There is hardly any effort to bring creativity in teaching.

As mentioned earlier a good teacher is too preoccupied with his task; completely committed and dedicated. Many of them would prefer to be loners than being a part of group of teacher politicians. Among these teacher politicians also need of being accepted by other colleagues does not seem to work. They would hardly care for the opinion of the other teacher. A hard bitter competition can be witnessed among them although on surface they may appear to be good colleagues. However the affiliation need can be found in the formation various teacher unions demanding pay hike and busy fighting with other union.

So in summary, the application of this theory to teaching profession is concerned, the theory has categorized human needs into three basic categories. As far as applicability of the theory to teaching profession is concerned it is said that the needs of achievement and power are getting stronger and stronger among teachers and the very important need of affiliation is going down in its importance. It would be very interesting to find out what is the true status as far as needs are concerned; Which need is strong and which need works relatively less.

Integrating the Content Theories

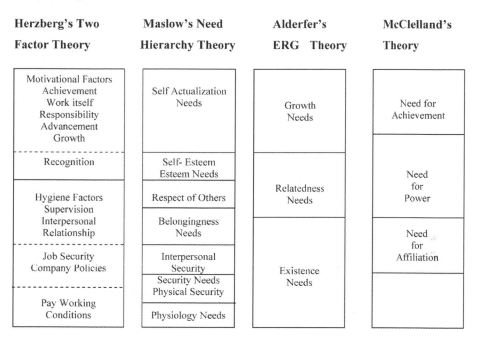

Fig. 1.9 Integrations of Content Theories

(Source: Gregary Moorhead and Ricky W.Griffin, Organizational Behaviour, p.146)

Murray's Manifest Needs

Another need theory is H.A. Murray's Manifest Need's theory. First presented by Murray in 1938, the theory identified two sets of needs, but only at an abstract level. Its present conceptualization owes much to the work of J.W. Atkinson, who translated Murray's ideas into a more concrete, operational framework. Murray proposed a greater variety of needs and believed that any number of needs might influence behavior at the same time.

Murray divided needs into two categories: (1) Psychogenic needs (abasement, achievement, affiliation etc. (2) Viscerogenic needs (food, water etc.). The psychogenic needs are those more closely identified with work motivation. Murray did not place the needs into any particular order of importance. He postulated that each need had two principal components direction and intensity. Direction deals with the object or person that is expected to satisfy the need. Intensity represents the relative importance of the need.

Appropriate environmental conditions are necessary for a need to become manifest. For example, if someone with a high need for power works in a job setting in which power is irrelevant, the need may remain latent not yet influencing the person's behavior but if conditionals that increase the importance of power arise, the need for power may then manifest itself and employees will begin to work towards increasing his or her power.

Little research has been done to evaluate Murray's theory. However, some of the specific needs defined by Murray have been the subject of much research.

Theory at a glance:

Murray has classified needs into 2 sets of categories. i.e. Psychogenic needs which implies achievement and affiliation and the other set is Viscerogenic needs (food, water etc.). Psychogenic needs are more important for work motivation, according to Murray. Psychogenic needs can be found similar to Maslow's higher order needs of love and belongingness, self esteem and self actualization or Herzberg's Motivational factors. Viscerogenic needs are similar to Maslow's lower order needs or safety and security and physiological needs or Herzberg's Hygiene factors. Murray has talked about direction and intensity of needs. Direction implies the need a person wishes to satisfy where as intensity implies to the force of the efforts to satisfy the need. Murray has said it is important to provide appropriate environment so that a person may feel like directing his efforts with intensity to satisfy the need. Little research has been done on Murray's theory of evaluation.

Application of the Theory to Teaching Profession

A teacher will try to satisfy both types of needs. However what has been a matter of concern is Viscerogenic needs are taking on Psychogenic needs. The teachers are behind fulfilling lower order of needs on account of many reasons. Many of the teachers are employed on clock hour basis due to government's ban on recruitment of new teachers. So one may find them hopping from one institute to the other conducting lectures. Other reason is being that as the ethical standards in the society itself has gone down and other professionals also are after making more and more money expecting teachers to remain aloof is quite unrealistic. The Viscerogenic needs which are considered to be very important for work motivation requires conducive working environment for a need to get manifested. The organizational environment can be mainly held responsible for the under performance of the teachers. It is said that our educational environment is "over-administered" and "under-led". Institutional climate in most of the institutions is closed and direct (or autocratic). The reward structure, is based on the number of completed years of service or contacts with political bosses which is highly demotivating for genuine, good teachers. Sycophants, nepotism and tide of manipulation rise, killing the creativity inside a genuine teacher. It is said the management councils or governing bodies also play the role of a villain in the drama of educational floundering. Overcrowded classrooms, lack of modern infrastructure, lack of research grants, insincere and undisciplined students and their unions tied to various political parties, complete apathy on the part of principal, director, VC to redress genuine problems of teachers; all what results in the Viscerogenic needs do not get manifested and genuine teachers completely feel alienated and disappointed with the system.

4 PROCESS THEORIES

Content theories emphasis the importance of inner needs in motivation. Maslow, Alderfer, Herzberg and other researchers focused on existence of these needs and their role in initiating the motivational cycle. Unfortunately, most content theories share three assumptions that limit their usefulness to managers. The theories assume that (1) all employees are alike (2) all situations are alike and (3) there is one best way to motivate all employees. In recent years, a substantially different approach to understanding motivation has emerged. The approach includes a number of process theories that view motivation as on individual's decision to act so as it put forth some given level of effort. There are three such theories, namely, Expectancy Theory, Equity Theory and Performance Satisfaction Model.

Expectancy Model

The Expectancy Model goes by several other names such as Instrumentality Theory, Path-Goal Theory and Valence—Instrumentality-Expectancy (VIE) Theory. The Expectancy Theory has its roots in the cognitive concepts of pioneering psychologists Kurt Lewin and Edward Tolman and in the choice behavior and utility concepts from classical economic theory. However, the first to formulate an expectancy theory directly aimed at work motivation was Victor H. Vroom.

Vroom's expectancy theory can be classified as a process theory in contrast to the content theory primarily because it attempts to identify relationships among variables in dynamic state as they affect individual behavior. This system orientation is in direct contrast to the content theories which have attempted largely to specific correlates of motivated behavior. In the expectancy theory, it is the relationship among inputs that is the basic focal point rather the inputs themselves.

Stated briefly, Vroom's expectancy model postulates that motivation depends on the strength of an expectation that the act will be followed by a given outcome and on the preference of an individual for that outcome. Fig.1.10 and fig 1.11 briefly summarize the expectancy theory.

There are three variables in the model which need elaboration.

Valence

Valence refers to the degree of desirability of outcomes as seen by the individual. In other words, valence refers to the strength of an individual's preference for a particular outcome. Other terms that might be used include value, incentive, attitude and expected utility.

Valence may vary from -1 to +1 as shown in fig.1.11. Valence is negative if the individual prefers not attaining an outcome compared with attaining it. Valence is 0, if he is indifferent to the outcome and valence is +1 if he has strong preference to the outcome. It goes without saying that the valence of the individual must be positive if motivation were to take place.

Instrumentality

Instrumentality refers to the belief that the first level outcome will lead to the second level outcome. For example, the person would be motivated towards superior performance because of the desire to be promoted. The superior performance (first level outcome) is seen as being instrumental in obtaining promotion (second-level outcome). In effect, the person makes a subjective judgment about the probability that the organization values the performance and will administer rewards suitably. The value of instrumentality varies from 0 to 1 (see Fig.1.11). If an employee sees that promotions are based on performance, instrumentality will be rated high. A low estimate of instrumentally will be made if the employee fails to see such linkage between performance and reward.

Expectancy:

Expectancy refers to the belief that an effort will lead to completion of a task. For example, a person selling magazine subscriptions door to door may know, from experience, that the volume of sales is directly related to the number of sales calls made. Expectancies stated as probabilities the employee's estimate of the degree to which performance will be determined by the amount of effort expend. Since expectancy is the probability of connection between effort and performance, its value may range from 0 to 1 (see Fig. 1.11). If an employee sees no chance that effort will lead to the desired performance, the expectancy is 0. On the hand, if he is confident that the task will be completed, the expectancy has a value of 1. Normally, the expectancies of employees will lie between these two extremes. Like valence, expectancy must also be high for motivation to take place.

At first glance, there appears to be no difference between expectancy and instrumentality. But expectancy is not the same as instrumentality. Expectancy, as was mentioned above, refers to the belief that the task will be performed. It is the first level outcome. Instrumentality, on the other hand, refers to the belief that the performance will result in the desired outcomes. In other words, it is the belief that the first-level outcome will lead to the second-level outcome. In summary, according to the expectancy theory motivation is—

Motivation=Expectancy X Instrumentality X Valance

This multiplicative relationship means that the motivational appeal of a give work path is drastically reduced whenever one or more of expectancy, instrumentality or valence approaches the value of zero. Conversely, for a given reward to have a high and positive motivational impact as a work outcome, the expectancy, instrumentality and valence associated with the reward must be high and positive.

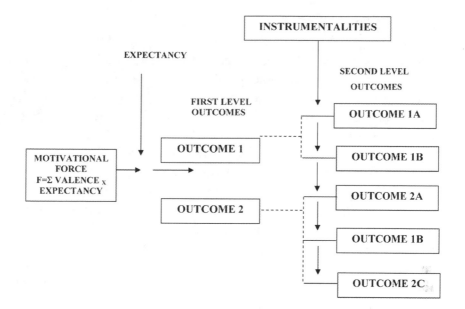

Fig. 1.10 Vroom's VIE Theory of Motivation

(Source: Fred Luthans, Organizational Behaviour, New York, McGraw-Hill, 1989, p.247)

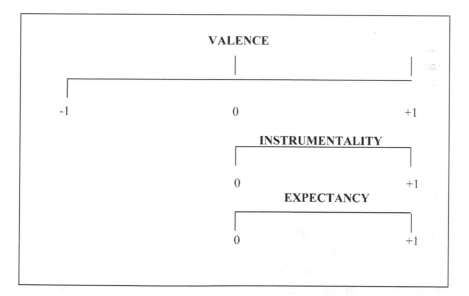

Fig. 1.11 Range of Valence, instrumentality and expectancy

(Source: K.Ashwathappa, Organizational behavior, p. 218)

Theory at a glance:

Unlike the content theories, this process theory tries to establish relationship among three complex variables i.e. Valence, instrumentality and Expectancy. Valence refers to an individual's preference to a desired outcome. In simple words, whether he likes a particular outcome; may be in the form of reward or not. Instrumentality refers to the instrument or medium or activity which leads to achieving expected reward or outcome. Expectancy refers to whether the individual believes that his efforts will result in achieving the outcome. According to Vroom, Valence can vary between -1 to +1. If it is -1, the person does not want to achieve or want particular outcome. If it is zero he is neutral and if it is +1 it shows strong desire on the part of individual to achieve the outcome. Instrumentality can vary between 0 to 1. If it is zero that means individual thinks that a particular medium will not lead to desired outcome; on the other hand if it is 1, then he strongly thinks that a particular activity will lead to desired outcome. Expectancy can vary between 0 to 1. If it is 0, the individual doesn't expect that his efforts will lead to a desired level of outcome and if it is 1 then the individual is very much optimistic about his efforts will lead to outcome. For a given outcome to become motivation for an employee, all three variables i.e. valence, instrumentality and expectancy must be high and positive.

Manager should firstly understand the needs of the employees and set the reward accordingly. It is said content theories can be of great help to understand employees' needs. Manager should select person with right abilities and try to provide conducive atmosphere for achieving the outcome. The relationship between performance and reward should be made clear at the onset itself to the employee.

Evaluation of the Expectancy Model

On the plus side, Vroom's proposed expectancy theory explains the complex relationship among various variables which results in motivation at the work place. The content theories had failed to explain the complex process of motivation. This theory has been quite a matter of research among academic circles.

Second, this theory is quite helpful in achieving both organizational as well as individual's needs. The first level of outcome can be the organizational goals, achievement of which lead to second level outcome that is individual goal.

Third, the expectancy theory is a cognitive theory because it views individual's actions are quite thoughtful and not merely to satisfy unmet needs or interest. So somewhere it preserves individual dignity.

Fourth, the expectancy theory goes beyond Maslow's or Herzberg's theories of Motivation. The theory states that the manager must create a conducive environment for the achievement of the outcome and should make the relationship between outcome and reward clear at the onset itself; so that employee's efforts can be directed towards rewards.

Despite its general appeal, this theory has also been criticized. The complex relationship among three variables is still open for questions. Still it needs to be found out to which situation the theory is applicable and to which it is not.

Second, the theory assumes that individuals make conscious or deliberate decision with much of thinking behind it. This can't be said to be true in case of routine work where there is little thinking behind it.

Third, although this theory is important, it is complex in nature and the testing of theory has not been done thoroughly and has been marginally successful. The theory also has its limitations to which situations it is applicable and to which it is not. For example, in situations where the relations between reward and performance are clear theory will work. However in jobs where rewards are based on seniority or some other criteria apart from performance this theory has no application.

Fourth, the model raised some fundamental questions. Will the complexity of theory make managers ignore it or pay attention only to its main points? Do managers have time in exploring various needs of large number of employees?

Despite its limitations theory has great value in understanding the complex concept of work motivation and the variables defined by the theory has great value for work motivation.

Application of the theory to Teaching Profession

As it is stated in its evaluation itself, the theory has got major limitation in its application to different situations. The theory demands conducive environment for the working of the relationship between three variables. That environment unfortunately seems to have not been there in our universities and institutions which are said to be "over-administered" and "under-led". It is said the organizational (or institutional) climate in most of the institutions is closed or autocratic. The reward structure, inside and outside the institutions, also militates against the genuine, silent and self-respecting teachers. The theory calls for making the reward and performance relationship clear at the onset itself. However the crux of the problem lies here in teaching profession. There is no relationship between performance and rewards. A teacher automatically gets reward after a certain number of years of service. The reward system in this profession has no bearing to performance. Rewards are given on any criteria apart from performance. So the application of this theory to teaching profession has serious limitations.

Equity Theory

The Equity Theory is another process theory. The theory owes its origin to several prominent theories like Festinger, Heider, Homans, Jacques, Patchen, Weick and Adams. However, it is Adams' formulation of the equity theory which is a highly developed and reached statement on the topic. Therefore, Adam's formulation is considered here.

Like any other theory, the equity theory is also alternatively known as the "Social Comparison" theory and "Inequity" theory. True to its name, the equity theory is based on the assumption that individuals are motivated by their desire to be equitably treated in their work relationships. When employees work for an organization, they basically exchange their services for pay and other benefits. The Equity Theory proposes that individuals attempt to reduce any inequity they may feel as a result of this exchange relationship. For example, if the employees feel that they are either overpaid or underpaid, the equity theory posits that they will be motivated to restore equity.

Four terms are important in the theory:

1. Person: The individual for whom equity or inequity exists.
2. Comparison other: Any group or individual used by a person as a referent regarding inputs and outcomes.
3. Inputs: Characteristics which individuals bring with them to the job: education, skills, experience and the like. These are subjectively perceived by a person.

4. Outcome: Pay, promotion and fringe benefits received from a job. These are also subjectively perceived by a person.

The theory proposes that the motivation to act develops after the person compares inputs/ outcomes with the identical ratio of the comparison other. Inequity is defined as the perception that person's job inputs/ outcomes ratio is not equal to the inputs/ outcomes ratio of the comparison other.

The basic equity proposal assumes that, upon feeling inequity, the person is motivated to reduce it. Further, the greater the felt inequity, the greater the motivation to reduce it.

When attempting to reduce inequity, the person may try a number of alternatives, some of which are:

1. Person altering his inputs.
2. Person altering his outcomes.
3. Person distorting his inputs and outcomes cognitively.
4. Person leaving the field.
5. Person trying to alter or cognitively distort input and outcomes of the comparison other or force him to leave the field.
6. Person changing the comparison other.

It is not that the person feeling inequity alone gets motivated to restore equity. He performs with a feeling of equity also gets motivated but to maintain the current situation.

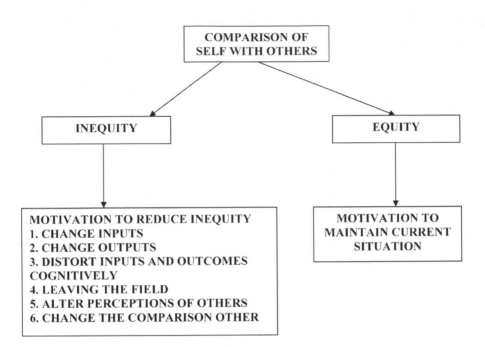

Fig. 1.12 Effect of equity and inequity on motivation

Theory at a glance:

This is a process theory which is based on comparison. A person working in any field always compares his inputs in terms of efforts with the outputs or rewards what he earns with that of other colleagues inputs and his rewards.

$$\frac{\text{Person's outcomes}}{\text{Person's Inputs}} = \frac{\text{Other's Outcomes}}{\text{Other's Inputs}}$$

Whenever he finds inequity, he tries to restore equity through various means. Like an employee feeling that he is underpaid compared to his another colleague for same amount of efforts may get demotivated and try to reduce his inputs i.e. efforts or may feel motivated and put in more efforts. He may change outputs like requesting for pay hike or bigger office or personal secretary. An employee can cognitively change the perception of input and outcomes. For example, an employee who feels that he is overpaid may start feeling that "yes I work harder than any other employee". Disappointed with injustice that he is not rewarded properly, he may totally leave the organization. He may change the perception of other; may console himself "he has better luck, he is close to the management or he is good in manipulating things and I don't want to do things what he is doing. I am fine at whatever I am doing". He can also change the referent person. Earlier he was comparing himself with A; now he starts comparing himself with B.

The theory not only motivates the person who perceives inequity but also motivates the person who perceives equity to maintain his efforts at the same level.

Evaluation of the Theory

Like any other theory of motivation, the equity theory has advantages and limitations.

On its positive side theory has lot of supportive research evidence and extensive amount of research has been done on this theory.

Secondly, the theory accepts the reality of social comparison. A man not only compares his inputs and rewards but what efforts others are putting and getting in return. Whenever he sees inequity he tries to reduce it by various means.

Third, theory considers the real nature of human beings that the world for a person is how he sees it or perceives it rather what is the actual reality. Maslow's theory was based upon individual needs and Herzberg's theory was based upon job context factors. But this theory takes into account the perception of the individual; what he "thinks" whether he is treated equally or unequally in terms of rewards with others. So it is not the actual situation but the perception of the individual which works while comparing himself with others. The research do suggests that most of the times, individuals overestimates the rewards of others.

The equity theory has its share of criticisms. The theory is based on the very foundation of equality of fair treatment what an individual perceives. So this is more applicable to mature employees who are in a position to judge the reality. An immature employee would always find himself under rewarded.

The theory is not clear about the areas mentioned below:

1. How to judge what is input and what are outcomes? Whether given "responsibility: is input or it is an "output"?
2. What are the criteria for choosing the person of comparison? And also what are the criteria for selecting a new person for comparison?
3. What are those circumstances which will make an individual to choose one alternative out of several available to reduce inequity? How does he choose a particular alternative?
4. The major criticism against the theory is that this is based on laboratory findings. Would it be applicable to organizational situations?

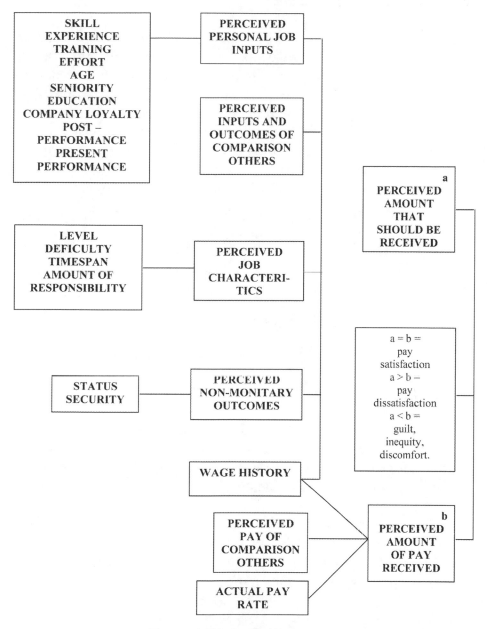

Fig. 1.13 Equity Components

(Source: H. John Bernardin and Joyce E.A.Rusell, Human Resource Management, New York, McGraw-Hill, 1993, p.422)

Managing the Equity Dynamic

Fig.1.14 shows that it would be the allocation of the rewards by the manager among subordinates which will affect the performance and job satisfaction of an employee. If an employee finds that he has got fair rewards compared to others, it will result in job satisfaction. If an employee feels manager has been unjust in giving him the rewards, it will result in employee's dissatisfaction. So the manager must make it sure, his acts are not seem by employees as unfair or favorable to a particular employee only. He should maintain proper balance and try to at least minimize the comparison which will be made in case of rewards.

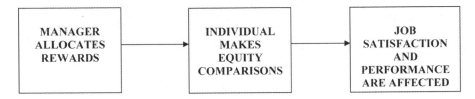

Fig. 1.14 The Equity Comparisons

There are two things which a manager should keep in mind:

1. Equity comparison is inevitable whenever visible rewards like pay, promotion are distributed.
2. He should anticipate the perceived inequity and be very effective in communicating the reasons and the elements he considered appropriate while distributing the rewards. The system of performance appraisal should be fair and transparent.

Manager should remember equity is the game of perception. How an individual perceives whether he is fairly treated or not. It is not what manager thinks whether he is right in distributing the rewards but the perception of the workers is important.

Application of the theory to the Teaching Profession:

This theory has its very significant application to the teaching profession. A teacher would all the time compare his rewards and efforts with that of other teacher's outcomes and his efforts and most of the time feel disappointed. Some teachers are found manipulating things to climb up the career ladder using political contacts and other unethical means and getting successful in achieving rewards without taking lectures or publishing a single research paper. It automatically demotivates a sincere and dedicated teacher who feels his efforts or intellectual abilities are of no use. At times such teacher can decide to leave the organization, depriving the students of the institute of a good teacher. If things reaches this far, the damage still remains restricted.

But seeing the means applied by one teacher for careerism the other teachers too, follow his footsteps. A teacher taking private tuitions even after being employed in institution, not taking lectures sincerely or not taking them at all, arriving late and going early and yet being successful in getting promotion, because he is close to management; may make the other sincere teachers feel frustrated and even they may decide to apply the same means. Teaching profession witnesses equity comparison in great intensity. The problem is with the distribution of rewards. They are based on seniority and every other criterion apart from merit. The system must be made credible and transparent where good performance should be the only criteria for getting reward.

Porter and Lawler's Performance-Satisfaction Model

Porter and Lawler came out with a comprehensive theory of motivation. They posit that motivation, performance and satisfaction are all separate variables and relate in ways different from what was traditionally assumed. Fig. 1.15 shows the multivariable model of Porter and Lawler. As shown in the figure, boxes 1,2 and 3 are basically the same as Vroom's equation. It is important, however, that Porter and Lawler point out that effort (force or motivation) does not directly lead to performance. It is mediated by abilities, traits and role perceptions. More important in the Porter and Lawler model is what happens after performance. The rewards that follow and how they are perceived, will determine satisfaction.

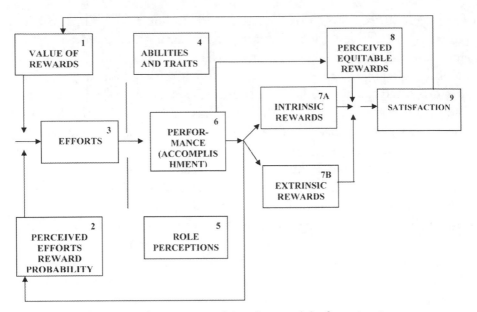

Fig.1.15 The Porter and Lawler model of motivation

Theory at a glance:

The theory includes the same variables as is being proposed by Victor Vroom. However according to Porter Lawler' model, the activity of performance is affected by the individual's abilities and traits and role perception. It leads to either intrinsic or extrinsic or either both types of rewards for person. If he finds the rewards are equitable i.e. fair compared with efforts, it leads to satisfaction. Otherwise he will be dissatisfied.

Evaluation of the Theory

Porter and Lawler's model offers some useful guidelines to the managers:

1. Chose right person for the job; seeing the abilities of the employees and requirements of the job.
2. Manager must clearly communicate the role what employee is expected to play and make it sure that he has understood his role.
3. Narrate in exact terms what level of performance is expected of the individual.

4. Manager must make it sure that the rewards are valued by the individual so that it will motivate him to achieve it.
5. The rewards distributed should be proportional to performance.

The Porter and Lawler model has definitely been able to explain the relationship between performance and satisfaction and the role played by perceived equitable rewards on intrinsic and extrinsic motivation. Like Vroom's Expectancy Theory, this theory is also criticized on the ground that all the efforts of an individual are not consciously decided. This is true especially in case of routine jobs. It is not the performance that leads to satisfaction. But sometimes it is the satisfaction which will lead to better performance. For example, if the worker gets praise for his work, he will work even harder to get more adulation. Finally there are many factors other than mentioned in the theory are responsible for motivation.

However due to its complexity it has no made so much impact as far as its applicability in Human Resource Management is concerned.

Applicability of the theory to the Teaching Profession

Like Victor Vroom's Expectancy Model, this theory also includes same variables. In teaching profession there is no relationship between performance and reward. So this theory too has similar limitations like Vroom's theory to the teaching profession.

5 SOME OTHER THEORIES / MODELS OF MOTIVATION

Reinforcement Theory

An influential and controversial approach to influencing human behavior is based on the observation that the consequences of an individual's behavior in one situation influence that individual's behavior in a similar situation in future. Techniques based on this principle have been developed to change human behavior. Such a technique, generally known as "operant conditioning", has been advocated by B.F. Skinner. Its implication is that individual behavior can be predicted, from a person's past experiences.

The operant conditioning approach to behavior is based on the law of effect, which states that behavior which has a rewarding consequence is likely to be repeated. There is positive reinforcement. On the other hand, a behavior that leads to negative or punishing consequence tends not to be repeated. There is negative reinforcement. When operant conditioning is used to control behavior of employees in an organization, it is called organizational behavior modification or OB Mod in its acronym.

The theory has an important implication to managers. If a manager desires to change the behavior of his subordinate, he (manager) must change the consequence of the behavior. An employee who frequently comes late can be motivated to come in on time if the manager expresses strong approval of each on time or early arrival, rather than shrugging the matter off. Late arrival can also be stopped by strongly disapproving such behavior. However, rewarding desirable behavior is more effective than punishing an undesired behavior. OB Mod uses four strategies to systematically reinforce desirable behavior while discouraging undesirable behavior.

These strategies are briefly discussed here:

1. **Positive Reinforcement:** It entails the use of rewards (or other positive consequences) that stimulates desired behavior and strengthens the probability of reporting such behavior in the future. Positive enforcers can be money, praise, promotion, recognition etc.

2. **Negative Reinforcement:** This strategy is also called "avoidance learning". It implies the use of unpleasant consequences to condition individuals to avoid behaving in undesirable ways. By making unpleasant consequences contingent on undesirable behavior, individuals learn to systematically change the patterns of behavior. Avoidance learning is not a strategy of punishment. We learn to watch for traffic crossing streets and to bundle up on cold days. Punishment or coercion is not implied in any of these actions. In work environments, training, safety warnings, orientation sessions and counseling help alert employees against negative consequences of undesirable behavior.

3. **Extinction:** There is withdrawal of all forms of reinforcement to remove or extinguish undesirable behavior. For instance, a disruptive employee who is punished by his supervisor for his undesirable behavior may continue the disruptions because of the attention they bring. By ignoring or isolating the disruptive employee, attention is withheld and possibly also the motivation for fighting.

4. **Punishment:** This tool is used when an unpleasant or undesirable behavior needs to be reduced or eliminated. For example, a worker's wages may be deducted if the quality of goods produced is of substandard quality.

Schedules of Reinforcement

1. **Fixed Interval schedules:** The time period of reward is fixed e.g. monthly.
2. **Variable interval schedules:** The time period of reward often varies, say, one time after 7 days, other time after 10 days.
3. **Fixed Ratio Schedule:** The reward is given after a fixed number of occurrences e.g. payment of Rs. 100 to a worker after he completes every five units of a product.
4. **Variable ratio schedule:** The reward is given, but the number of occurrences is not fixed.

A counterpoint to Goal-Setting Theory is Reinforcement Theory. The former is a cognitive approach, proposing that an individual's purpose direct his or her action. In Reinforcement Theory, we have a behaviorist approach, which argues that reinforcement conditions behavior. The two are clearly at odds philosophically. Reinforcement theorists see behavior as being environmentally caused. You need not be concerned, they would argue, with internal cognitive events; what controls behavior are reinforcers—any consequence that, when immediately following a response, increases the probability that the behavior will be repeated.

Theory at a glance:

According to Reinforcement Theory, a behavior which has got positive consequences is likely to be repeated and the behaviors which has negative consequences is not likely to be repeated. The past experience with a particular behavior can lead to prediction of behavior. These techniques are called operant conditioning. These principles are being advocated by B.F. Skinner. The behavior which leads to positive consequences in the form of reward or praise is likely to be repeated. This is called "positive reinforcement" and the behavior which likely to be resulted in negative consequences like punishment is not likely to be repeated. This is called "negative reinforcement". If these principles are used in the organization set up to change the behavior of employee it is called Organizational Behavior Modification or OB Mod. A manager who wishes to change the behavior of employee must change the consequences accordingly. The policy of reward or praise i.e. positive reinforcement would always prove effective than negative reinforcements. There are various strategies to apply reinforcement. Positive reinforcement results in reward or praise. Negative reinforcement does not mean any kind of punishment but it is avoidance learning i.e. a person learns to avoid a particular set of behavior. Organizing safety training or counseling programs are the examples in the organization of negative reinforcements. Extinction means withdrawal of all kinds of reinforcements so that the behavior automatically gets extinguished and finally there is punishment which is used in case of unpleasant behavior. The schedules of reinforcements can be in the form of fixed or variable.

Evaluation of the Theory:

All though Reinforcement Theory is of importance in analyzing the behavior; however many researchers have argued that typically speaking this is not the theory of motivation because it does not explain what caused the behavior at the first place itself. However it is of great help in controlling the behavior. So it has become a part of discussion of motivation. However the theory completely ignores the inner state of human beings.

The theory gives considerable insight into how people learn. It is a powerful motivation device. But it ignores feelings, attitudes, expectations and other cognitive variables which are also strong in having effect on behavior.

Reinforcement is not the only one influence on behavior. In terms of organizational behavior apart from reinforcements, it is also affected by goals, inequity and expectations.

Application of the theory to the Teaching Profession:

The theory has limited impact as far as teaching profession is concerned. The tragedy is that there are no reiforcers for a teacher that his positive behavior being praised or rewarded. As far as negative reinforcers are concerned they are hardly used like taking action against a teacher for nor conducting the classes regularly or action against his late arrival regularly. Even if the college principle decides to ignore a particular teacher for his late arrival, the teacher's behavior does not get extinguished; in fact it may rise even more. At times a negative reinforcer may lead to complete drastic action on the part of teacher as high as leaving the institution altogether. This is a profession where employees seek autonomy but don't like being held accountable for it. On the other hand, there are those committed teachers who complain that there are hardly any positive reinforcers for good performance. Increments or promotion is based on certain number of completed years of service and not the effect of good performance as a teacher. A teacher's behavior is affected by many other variables apart from reinforcers so the theory has very marginal application to the teaching profession.

Cognitive Evaluation Theory

According to one of the researchers, introduction of extrinsic rewards like pay for work goes on reducing the intrinsic reward which the person enjoys from the work which he / she performs. This proposal of late 1960s is called as Cognitive Evaluation Theory. This study has been a matter of interest for many researchers and many studies do in fact support this theory.

Historically, motivation theorists made a clear distinction between intrinsic motivations a person enjoys due to achievement, responsibility and competence and extrinsic motivation a person gets due to high pay, promotions, good supervisor relations, and pleasant working conditions. Both were considered independent. That is, change in one will not affect the other. But the Cognitive Evaluation Theory contradicts this assumption. It states that when organizations use extrinsic rewards like pay for performance, the intrinsic rewards, enjoyed by individuals for doing what they like to do, go on reducing.

The reason for it is that the individual can no more remain in control of his own behavior but his behavior is driven by the pressure to earn external rewards. On the other hand, if extrinsic rewards are removed, one can find change in perception of an individual about why he or she does a particular task.

Although many studies support this theory, it is also criticized due to methodology used in these studies and in the interpretation of the findings. Still there is lot of ambiguity about whether extrinsic rewards reduce intrinsic motivation. A definite "yes" or "no" still can not be predicted.

Theory at a glance:

According to the theory the extrinsic rewards when offered go on reducing internal satisfaction. This happens because the person finds loss of control over situation. For example, an actor in his struggling time enjoys his work and it gives him intrinsic satisfaction although the extrinsic rewards associated with are very low. But once he becomes star, according to this theory, the intrinsic satisfaction from the content of work itself go on reducing. Earlier it was assumed that there is no relation between intrinsic motivations like responsibility, achievement etc and extrinsic motivators like pay, promotion, incentives. But according to this theory, there exists a definite relation between the two. Extrinsic motivators like pay off for high performance go on reducing intrinsic motivation.

If this hold validity, it has got major implications for the managers. Earlier there has been strong advocacy on the part compensation specialist that pay should be made contingent upon performance. However the Cognitive Evaluation Theory argues that doing so would lead to reducing individual's intrinsic motivation.

Evaluation of the Theory:

Although the research has suggested the interdependence of intrinsic and extrinsic motivation, the theory calls for more research to clear the ambiguity. However its impact on work motivation is found to be less than what was thought about general motivation. Many researchers have attacked the methodology used for the research. Most of the research has been done with students rather than employees; trying to find out the behavior of the students if a reward is stopped. But it is not typical work situation. In real life situation an employee may strongly resists for withdrawal of extrinsic reward. Even if the job itself is interesting there is still expectation of employee that there should be some extrinsic reward for the performance. On the other hand, on a dull job, extrinsic rewards increase intrinsic motivation. Therefore, the theory may have limited applicability to work organizations because most low-level jobs are not inherently satisfying enough to foster high intrinsic interest and many managerial and professional positions offer extrinsic rewards. Therefore it is said that Cognitive Evaluation Theory may be relevant to that set of organizational jobs that falls in between—those that are neither extremely dull nor extremely interesting.

Application of the Theory to the Teaching Profession:

In earlier times the teachers used to get high intrinsic motivation from the job of teaching itself and the esteem associated with it. They hardly bothered for extrinsic rewards associated with the job. However with the changed times, like other professions, intrinsic satisfaction has not remained sufficient. Teachers too demand good extrinsic rewards. With the passage of time there has been in fact demand for better and better extrinsic rewards; denial of it sometimes has resulted in reduction of intrinsic job satisfaction. One can not say commercialization of education system has resulted in loss of intrinsic motivation among teachers. i.e. extrinsic rewards are responsible for reduction in intrinsic satisfaction. If that has been the case, the western education system is highly commercialized. There are very high extrinsic rewards associated with the job of teaching. But there is no significant evidence to suggest that intrinsic motivation has gone down. One must understand the reality, like any other profession teaching too is a profession wherein people working are like any other human beings. They require money for their living being. So any withdrawal of extrinsic reward would infact result in complete elimination of intrinsic motivation which is already at a low point.

Proponents of Cognitive Evaluation Theory say that pay should not be based on performance as pay being extrinsic reduces intrinsic satisfaction. However there have many voices from the experts to make pay based on performance to increase performance of teachers. It is true that there has been decrease in intrinsic motivation of teachers, but reasons are certainly other than introduction of extrinsic rewards

Goal-Setting Theory

In the late 1960s, Edwin Locke proposed the theory of goal setting in the late 1960s. According to him setting a specific goal i.e. telling employee explicitly what has to be achieved and what needs to be done to achieve it, can result in employee expanding his efforts. The value of goals can not be overlooked. Specific goals rather than vague, little difficult goals than easy one and goals with feedback rather than no feedback, can certainly increase motivation.

Specific difficult goal when accepted by an individual can produce more outputs than a very general goal of "do your best". According to this theory, feedback is also very important in order to motivate an employee to exert more efforts. Feedback acts as a guide as it lets an individual know how he is progressing and can make him know the gap between the expected and actual status. That too, self-generated feedback rather than feedback given by some other person has more influence in motivating an individual. Still there is no clarity about role of employee participation in goal setting. Some studies suggests if employee is involved in setting goal, he feels more motivated, while other studies suggest employees doing well when the goals are assigned by the superiors. However it is to be noted that employee's acceptance becomes easier when he is involved in the process of setting the goal. Employees are more likely to resists the difficult goal which is assigned to him without even discussing with him.

There are four other factors have been found to influence the goals-performance relationship. They are goal commitment, adequate self efficacy, task characteristics, and national culture.

Goal commitment is the determination on the part of an employee not to lower or abandon the goal till it is achieved. Self-efficacy is the confidence to succeed in the task. It is individual's belief in his own abilities. People with low self-efficacy are likely to reduce their efforts or give up the goal altogether. People with high self-efficacy also respond positively after getting a negative feedback by putting more efforts and opposite can be found with low self efficacy people. Task characteristics assumes that little difficult goals which make an employee stretch his efforts will produce better result than a very easy goal. It is an obvious scenario that easy goals are likely to be more accepted than difficult goals but once the individual accepts the difficult goals and has all the competence to perform the task, it can result in higher productivity. This theory stands strong in case of North American culture and less applicable in Asian culture where people normally are found to dislike specificity.

Theory at a glance:

According to the Goal Setting Theory, specifically set goals lead to higher performance rather than generalized goals like do your best. Difficult goals result in higher performance rather than easy goals. Although easy goals are likely to be accepted easily; difficult goals when accepted leads to higher performance. Feedback to the performance acts as a stimulus. However self generated feedback, whereby employee himself can monitor his own work will work as more effective feedback than externally generated feedback. Participation of employee in setting goal is important or not; the results are mixed on this. However difficult goals are more likely to be accepted if the employee has participation in goal setting process. There are four more characteristics that are important. They are goal commitment, self-efficacy, task characteristics and national culture. A person should have strong goal commitment to achieve the goal. Self-efficacy is the belief the person has in himself that he can achieve a particular goal. Task characteristic is the nature of the goal. If the task is simple than complex, well learned than novel and independent than interdependent, it will result in higher motivation. The theory is more applicable to the western culture where power distance is high and uncertainty avoidance is low.

Evaluation of Goal Setting Theory

Research indicates that individual goal setting doesn't work equally well on all tasks. The evidence suggests that goals seem to have a more substantial effect on performance when tasks are simple rather than complex, well-learned rather than novel, and independent rather than interdependent. On interdependent tasks, group goals are preferable. Finally, goal-setting theory is culture bound. It's well adapted to countries like the United States and Canada because its key components align reasonably well with North American cultures. It assumes that employees will be reasonably independent (not too high a score on power distance), that managers and employees will seek challenging goals (low in uncertainty avoidance), and that performance is considered important by both (high in quantity of life). So this theory may not necessarily lead to higher employee performance in countries such as Portugal or Chile, where the opposite conditions exist.

Overall conclusion can be that intentions—as articulated in terms of hard and specific goals—are a potent motivating force. Under the proper conditions, they can lead to higher performance. However, there is no evidence that such goals are associated with increased job satisfaction.

Application of the Theory to the Teaching Profession:

The theory has little relevance to the teaching profession. Goals should specific. Today's teachers do not have any specific goals apart from taking certain number of lectures per week. This work is also hampered on account of different reasons like holidays, non availability of the classroom on account of different reasons. To add to the worse, one would hardly find any goal commitment on the part of the teachers. They come late for the classes, leave early and sometimes do not engage classes. The theory says difficult goals lead to high performance than easy one and participation of employee in setting goal can result in higher performance. Whether it is difficult goal or simple goal, a teacher hardly has got any participation in setting the goal. According to the theory feedback to the performance increases the performance. However a teacher gets no feedback to his performance or one can say that there is no system in place for evaluating performance of the teacher. In fact teachers do not want their work to be evaluated by the principal or director, peers, students or even by themselves. Some of the teachers go on just dictating notes years after years from the same old notebook, the element of self efficacy seem to be very less among such teachers. Task characteristics can also be a motivator for the employee. However in a teacher's job one would hardly find any novelty; although he gets promoted from the post of lecturer to the assistant professor or professor, his duties and responsibilities almost remain the same. There should be more efforts to make a teacher's job challenging or interesting one by making him the owner of the process. Right from setting the syllabus, to conducting exams and giving feedback to the students on their performance in the exams, the teacher should be made in charge of this responsibility. This practice is already being there in IIMS and IITs. But applicability of it to rest of the educational institutions may end up creating more mess for the system of education.

Hackman-Oldham Job Characteristics Model:

Richard Hackman and Greg Oldham have shown that there are five job characteristics which lead to three psychological states which in turn affect the motivation and satisfaction of the employees. They also emphasize the fact that this entire cycle of relationship is moderated by the strength of the growth need on the part of an employee.

The five job characteristics which are central to provide potential motivation to workers are: skill variety, task identity, task significance, autonomy and feed back from the job itself. According to Hackman and Oldham, skill variety, task identity and task significance influence 'experienced meaningfulness'. Autonomy affects the 'experienced responsibility' or the feelings of being in control and being responsible for outcome. Feedback influences experienced knowledge of results' or the satisfaction of knowing how well one is. Skill variety notes the extent to which any particular job utilizes a range of skills, abilities and talents of employees. Obviously, if many different skills are used by the employee on the job, the job is going to provide challenge and growth experience to the employee.

Task identity indicates the extent to which the job involves a "whole" and identifiable piece of work. If the job involves beginning an assignment and completing it then the individual can identify with the ultimate creation turned out by him and derive pride and satisfaction from having done a worthwhile job.

Task significance refers to the meaningfulness or significance of the impact that a job has on the lives of others-both inside and outside the organization. If what one does has an impact on the well being of others, the job becomes psychologically rewarding to the person who performs it.

Autonomy reflects the extent to which the job provides an employee freedom, independence and discretion to schedule the work and make decisions and formulate the procedures to get the job done without interference from others. The greater the degree of autonomy, the more the person feels "in control". Since the employee has more freedom to perform the job, this autonomy will provide him with both the motivation to do the job and the satisfaction from doing it. Feedback indicates the extent to which the persons who are working on the job can assess whether they are doing things right or wrong even as they perform the job. The job itself provides this kind of feedback on how well they are reforming.

Thus, all these three experienced psychological states emanate from the intrinsic work rewards experienced by the employee which will result in high intrinsic motivation, high quality of work performance, high levels of job satisfaction, high job involvement, and lower absenteeism and turnover.

Hackman and Oldham state that only those who have a high growth need strength (that is the need to learn, develop and grow on the job) will experience the critical psychological states when the five core job characteristics are embedded in their work and experience the positive outcomes. Those who do not have high growth needs will not be affected by the mere job characteristics. That is, even if the job is enriched, involvement, satisfaction and performance levels will not change.

MPS: Motivation Potential Score
According to Hackman and Oldham, the propensity of each job to be motivating can be assessed by using the formula:

$$\text{MPS} = \frac{(\text{Skill Variety} + \text{Task Identity} + \text{Task Significance})}{3} \times \text{Autonomy} \times \text{Feedback}$$

According to this model, the first three characteristics have an additive relationship. Thus they may compensate for each other. More in one may compensate for deficit in other. However, autonomy and feedback have multiple relationships with other three characteristics.

It may be noted that because of the multiplicative effects of the model, if either autonomy or feedback happens to be totally absent in the job, then the job will have no motivating potential at all.

Theory at a glance:

According Richard Hackman and Greg Oldham, there are five job characteristics which lead to the motivation and job satisfaction. However, at the on set itself, the theory makes it clear that it applies to those employees in whom growth needs are found to be high; those employees who want to learn, develop and grow on the job. The five job characteristics are: skill variety, task identity, task significance, autonomy and feed back from the job itself. If the job requires skill variety it will provide challenge and learning experience to the worker. Task identity is the work or part of work performed by the worker. If the worker is in complete charge of the process, he feels satisfied about the creation turned on by him and it creates a pride in him. Task significance is the importance of the job or the impact it has on the lives of people inside or outside the organization. Autonomy refers to the independence or freedom or discretion a person has got in scheduling his job or taking decisions regarding it. Feedback provides the worker how well he is working on the job. Hackman and Oldham have given a formula also for calculating motivational potential score. According to them skill variety, task identity and task significance have additive effect and they can compensate for each other. However any lack of autonomy or feedback can result in eliminating motivational potential in the job.

As the theory is applicable to the employees having high order growth needs, it will not affect motivation of employees in whom growth needs are low or absent. All the efforts to enrich the job of such employees will result in futility.

Application of the Theory to the Teaching Profession:

The theory has great relevance for the profession of teaching. Teaching profession has got all the characteristics which have additive effect. i.e. it demands skill variety, it has task significance and task identity. The teachers in India today lack the other two important elements which have significant bearing on the motivational potential. i.e. autonomy and feedback. As one would see especially in government aided institutions there are more bureaucratic hurdles which a high growth oriented teacher will not like. There has been case, where one of the eminent faculty members of IIM Ahmedabad leaving the job because of the kind of delay he faced for approval for his research project from the government. The element of autonomy is completely restricted in teaching profession. Other significant variable of feedback is also missing in teaching profession. A teacher would hardly get to know how he is doing on job.

In case of teaching profession, two aspects of autonomy and feedback need to be given more attention to increase the motivation potential. Task identity element can also be improved by making teacher owner of the complete process; right from setting syllabus to giving feedback to students on their performance in the exams. However one must keep in mind that this theory is only applicable to those employees who are high growth oriented and want to learn and develop themselves.

Teachers having average skills and interest may infact resist the challenging work.

The Flow Experience

A key element of the flow experience is that its motivation is unrelated to end goals. The activity people are pursuing when they achieve the timelessness feeling of flow comes from the process of the activity itself rather than trying to reach a goal. So when a person experiences flow, he or she is completely intrinsically motivated.

Do people typically feel happy when they're experiencing flow? The answer, which might surprise you, is No. They're too consumed in deep concentration. But when the flow task is completed, and the person looks back on what has happened, he or she is flooded with feelings of gratitude for the experience. It's then that the satisfaction received from the experience is realized. And it is the desire to repeat the experience that creates continued motivation.

Are there conditions that are likely to produce flow? Yes. When people have described flow experiences, they talked about common characteristics in the tasks they were doing. The tasks were challenging and required using a high level of skills. They were goal-directed and had feedback on how well they were performing. The tasks demanded total concentration and creativity. And the tasks were so consuming that people had no attention left over to think about anything irrelevant or to worry about problems. However it is to be noted again, though, that although the task was goal-directed, it wasn't the goal that provided the motivation. It was the task.

One of the most surprising research findings related to flow is that it's not associated with leisure. The flow experience, in fact, is rarely reported by people when they're doing leisure activities such as watching television or relaxing. Another surprise is that it's more likely to be experienced at work than at home.

If you ask people if they'd like to work less, the answer is almost always Yes. People link leisure with happiness. They think if they had more free time, they'd be happier. Studies of thousands of people suggests that people are generally wrong in this belief. When people spend time at home for instance, they often lack a clear purpose, don't know how well they're doing, get distracted, and feel that their skills are underused. They frequently describe themselves as bored. But work has many of the properties that stimulate flow. It usually has clear goals. It provides people with feedback on how well they're doing—either from the work process itself or through a boss's evaluation. People's skills are typically matched to their jobs which provide challenge. And job usually encourage concentration and prevent distractions.

Theory at a glance:

According to the theory, it is not the goal but the process of achieving the goal, gives a human being intrinsic satisfaction. These people will not feel happy when the process is going on because they are completely engrossed and concentrated in the activity and don't have time to think about the process. But once the process is completed, when they look back at it, it gives them immense pleasure and this pleasure makes them repeat the process again. People experiencing such pleasure have stated the task characteristics. The tasks are challenging and creative and require high level of skills, goal directed and give feedback. Although the task was goal directed, it was not the goal but the process of achieving the goal gave satisfaction to the individual.

There are also some interesting findings. According to the study, the equation of happiness with leisure is wrong. People do not get the same pleasurable experience at the time leisure. They feel happier at work rather than at home because they find themselves doing nothing, their skills are not used and they lack clear purpose. However on the job, their efforts are concentrated and directed and they get self feedback or from the boss. Their skills are also used. So the process becomes an experience of pleasure.

Application to the Teaching Profession:

The theory does have application to the teaching profession. Highly dedicated and growth oriented people do get pleasure from the process of passing on knowledge. His real goal is completing certain number of lectures per week. But the preparation for the lecture and delivering the lecture in front of sincere students can give immense pleasure to a dedicated teacher. The attendance of number of students present and their reactions and respect for him, can work as the feedback for the work. Delivering the lecture calls for number of skills and creativity. So the process of delivering lecture itself can give the teacher immense happiness.

Theory does have certain applicability to the profession of teaching.

A Model of Intrinsic Motivation

A clearer understanding of flow has been offered in Ken Thomas's model of intrinsic motivation. This extension of the flow concept identifies the key elements that create intrinsic motivation. Thomas describes employees as intrinsically motivated when they genuinely care about their work, look for better ways to do it, and are energized and fulfilled by doing it well. As with flow, the rewards an employee gets from intrinsic motivation comes from the work itself rather than from external factors like increases in pay or compliments from the boss.

Thomas's model proposes that intrinsic motivation is achieved when people experience feelings of choice, competence, meaningfulness and progress. He defines these components as follows.

- Choice is the opportunity to be able to select task activities that make sense to you and to perform them in ways that seem appropriate.
- Competence is the accomplishment you feel in skillfully performing task activities you've chosen.
- Meaningfulness is the opportunity to pursue a worthy task purpose; a purpose that matters in the larger scheme of things.
- Progress is feeling that you're making significant advancement in achieving the task's purpose.

Thomas reports a number of studies demonstrating that these four components of intrinsic motivation are significantly related to improved job satisfaction and increased performance as rated by supervisors. However, almost all the studies reported by Thomas were done with professional and managerial employees. Whether these four components will predict intrinsic motivation, for example, rank-and-file blue-collar workers, is currently unclear.

It is interesting to see how Thomas's four intrinsic motivation components link with the concept of flow. When a task is meaningful, people find themselves resenting the time they have to spend on other less meaningful tasks. They're totally absorbed in the intrinsic task, thinking about it all the time. We should even expect them to borrow time from other activities in order to devote more time to something that's meaningful. When a task provides a flow experience a person typically is free to choose work on that task in contrast to others. Competence also stimulates the flow experience. We tend to be "most engaged in a task when we are performing activities most completely—having all our attention on meeting the challenge of the activities we are performing." Finally, progress enhances feelings that our time and efforts are paying off. You feel enthusiastic about the task and are eager to keep investing your time and effort in it.

Theory at a glance:

Model of Intrinsic Motivation has been offered by Ken Thomas. According to Thomas an employee feels intrinsically motivated when he cares for work, finds better ways of doing the work and is energized. The intrinsic satisfaction that he gets from the job matters to him than extrinsic reward of pay or praise by the boss. The model has proposed four components i.e. choice—to select an activity, Competence—skillfully performing task, Meaningfulness—worthy task, Progress—significant advancement. The components are related to each other in an interesting way. A person chooses a task which he finds meaningful. The satisfaction he gets from performing it makes him borrow time even from the other activities. His competence in doing the task makes him feel more motivated leading to progress where he can realize his efforts are really paying off. He feels happy about the task and keeps on investing his time and efforts in it.

Application of the Theory to the Teaching Profession:

This theory also applies to the teaching profession. Its only when the teacher finds his task meaningful, he would invest his efforts, time and creativity in performing the task. But in case of dedicated and true teachers, this model is certainly applicable. The choice of selecting the task or what we can call as autonomy is important for him. He finds his task very meaningful and worthy and gets fully concentrated at times sacrificing even the time required for domestic purposes. He has competence and because of which he finds himself progressing well in his task. It keeps on giving happiness and keeps him involved in the task. But how many teachers find their job meaningful is also a matter of research. How many of them have chosen the profession out of will or as a final option needs to be found out. How many teachers really have got the competence to perform the task, it is also a big question.

Attribution Theory

Attribution theory differs from the other theories of motivation because it identifies attributions made by people as the basis for their motivation. Attribution theory does not just explain individual motivation but explains the relationship between personal perception and interpersonal behavior. Although there are many attribution theories, all of them share common assumptions:
  i)   They try to provide a logical explanation to all that is happening.
  ii) They attribute actions of individuals to internal or external causes.
  iii) These theories propose that individuals follow a fairly logical approach in making attributions.

According to Harold H. Kelley, a famous social psychologist, attribution theory deals with the cognitive processes of an individual, which help interpret his behavior as being caused by aspects pertaining to the relevant environment. Attribution theory tries to answer the "why" aspect of motivation and behavior. The theory states that since the causes and reasons for an individual's cannot be directly observed, one has to depend to a great extent on the perception of the individual in order to understand his behavior. Attribution theory also assumes that humans are rational and motivated beings. This inherent nature of human beings makes them identify and understand the reasons for everything that takes place in their environment.

Many cognitive theories contributed to the development of Attribution theory, but the credit for initiating it goes to Friz Heider. According to Heider, behavior is determined by both internal forces or personality attributes such as ability, effort and fatigue and external forces or environmental attributes such as rules, weather etc. He emphasizes that it is the perceived attributes of an individual, which are important in determining the individual's behavior and not the actual attributes. The behavior of people when they perceive the internal attributes of an individual differs from their behavior when they perceive the external attributes associated with the individual. This concept of differential attribution has very important implications for work motivation.

Theory at a glance:

Attribution theory identifies attributions or reasons given by individuals for their motivation. It explains not only the basis of motivation but also the relationship between individual's perception and his behavior. There are many attribution theories. But all of them have some common assumptions. They try to provide logical explanation to what is happening. According to these theories individual behavior is guided by external or internal causes and individual follow quite logical approach in making attributions. Attribution theory tries to answer "why" answer behind individual's behavior and motivation. According to the theory causes and reasons for an individual's behavior can not be observed directly. One has to find out individual's perception for the reason. According to the perception of individual he makes sense of the environment around him and behaves accordingly.

According to Heider, behavior is generated by both internal and external forces. It is the perceived attributes of the individual not the actual ones which determine his behavior. Sometimes the behavior of a person quite differs from internal attributes of individual. At such time it can be said to be on account of external forces. This concept of differential attribution has very important implications for work motivation.

Locus of Control Attributions:

'Locus of control' refers to the chief source of factors that creates a result or gives rise to an outcome in the employee's perception. The outcome or result could depend on either external factors or internal factors. An understanding of the locus of control as perceived by various employees helps in a better understanding of their behavior at work. Those employees who believe that there is an internal control for all outcomes feel that they have the power to change or influence the outcomes by means of their ability, skills and efforts. But, those employees who believe that there is an external control for all outcomes feel that they are in no position to control them. In their opinion, external factors like luck, chances etc. are responsible for influencing outcomes. An employee's perceived locus of control is important in determining his/her own performance and satisfaction level.

Several researchers have studied employee behavior in terms of the Attribution Theory locus of control model in work settings. It has been found that employees with an internal locus of control are usually happier in their jobs, occupy managerial positions and prefer the participatory style of management as compared with employees with an external locus of control. Managers with an internal locus of control are in general, better performers, considerate towards their subordinates are not over-stressed and follow a strategic approach. Although many studies reveal that employees with an internal locus of control are better than their counterparts having an external locus of control, there is contradictory evidence from other studies. For instance, some studies find that managers with an external locus of control are perceived to take more initiative and be more considerate than managers with an internal locus of control.

Other Attributions

As explained earlier, attribution theory helps in a better understanding of organizational behavior. Therefore, other aspects of attribution by employees are being studied in order to extend the scope of the theory. Bernard Weiner, a social psychologist, found that the stability of attribution was also important in determining motivation. According to Weiner, employees with longer work experience tend to have stable internal attributions about their abilities and unstable internal attributions regarding effort. These employees also usually have stable external attributions regarding the task difficulty and unstable external attributions regarding luck.

Kelley suggested other dimensions such as consensus, consistency and distinctiveness having an impact on the type of attributions made by individuals. Consensus denotes the extent to which others behave in a similar manner in the same situation. The second dimension, consistency refers to a pattern of behavior, which may be relatively stable or unstable. This shows whether a person behaves similarly in a similar situation or if a particular behavior is just an infrequent occurrence. Distinctiveness indicates whether a person's behavior is similar for all tasks or whether his behavior differs from one task to another. Hence, it can be said that distinctiveness pertains to other tasks, consensus pertains to other people and consistency pertains to time. An individual having high consensus, consistency, as well as distinctiveness can be expected to make attributions to external or environmental factors. However, individuals showing low consensus, high consistency and low distinctiveness, can be expected to attribute outcomes or results to internal or personal causes.

Weiner used Attribution theory to explain achievement motivation and also to predict how people feel about themselves and their performance. Some of his findings are described below:

- Bad-luck attributions i.e. when people blame their failures to external causes like bad luck, fate etc., it helps reduce the pain and disappointed associated with failure.
- At the other extreme, good-luck attributions or attributing success to factors like good luck, chance etc. reduce the happiness associated with the success.
- When people attribute their success to internal factors, their expectations of success in the future tend to be higher. They set challenging goals for performance and have desire for achievement.

A study of the attribution theory can help managers to become aware of the attribution processes of individuals and how it affects their behavior in the organization. The managers can reinforce the belief in their subordinates that their success and progress in the organization is an outcome of their own efforts and abilities. At the same time, they can discourage employee from attributing to external causes such as difficulty of the task or bad luck.

Theory at a glance:

Locus of control is the chief factor in determining employee's performance. Those employees who have got internal locus of control for all outcomes feel that they can change the output by their abilities, skill and hard work. On the other hand, those employees having external locus of control, according to them luck, chance etc are responsible for influencing the outcome.

The results of the research are mixed with satisfaction and employees locus of control. Some studies found that employees with high internal locus of control are happier on their jobs and occupy managerial positions and have a strategy for their action. On the other hand, managers with external locus of control are considerate towards subordinates and take more initiative.

Locus of control theory is helpful in explaining goal setting behavior, leadership behavior and employee behavior. Further process of attribution plays an important role in formation coalition in the organization.

In other attributions, Weiner says that stability of attribution is also important. Employees with longer work experience have stable internal locus of control regarding their abilities and unstable internal attributions regarding their efforts.

Another researcher Kelly has suggested dimensions like consensus, consistency and distinctiveness, Consensus denotes the extent to which others behave in a similar manner in the same situation. The second dimension, consistency refers whether a person behaves similarly in a similar situation or if a particular behavior is just an infrequent occurrence. Distinctiveness indicates whether a person's behavior is similar for all tasks or whether his behavior differs from one task to another. An individual having high consensus, consistency, as well as distinctiveness can be expected to make attributions to external or environmental factors. However, individuals showing low consensus, high consistency and low distinctiveness, can be expected to attribute outcomes or results to internal or personal causes. Weiner has also used the theory to explain how people predict about their performance and its attribution. People attributing performance to bad luck tries to reduce the pain associated with failure. On the other hand, attributions like good luck or chance reduces happiness associated with it. When people attribute their success to internal locus of control, their expectation about success tends to be higher and they set challenging goals for themselves.

So the task in front of manager is to boost the confidence of the employees that their success is the result of their own abilities and efforts and discourage employees from attributing it to bad luck or task difficulty.

Application of the Theory to the Teaching Profession:

Research can be conducted on hypothesis that high or good performing teachers are found to be having high internal locus of control. On the other hand, those of average or poor performance have got external locus of control, many times attributing their bad performance to insincere students, crowded classrooms, unsupportive management, institutional environment etc. This hypothesis can be tested in the research.

6 OTHER EMERGING THEORIES

Control Theory:

Apart from the theories of motivation that are based on cognitive psychology, there are other theories, such Control Theory and Agency theory, which have become popular in recent times.

There are two versions of the control theory. One version states that control is a cognitive phenomenon. It reflects an individual's ability to control his life and aspects associated with his job. Recent studies reveal people who have personal control are able to handle unpleasant events with poise and experience less stress as compared to the individuals who lack such personal control. It has also been proved that such perceived control enhances job satisfaction and reduces absenteeism.

The other version of the control theory focuses on the control function, which is an integral part of the management process. While traditional theories consider control of both the inputs and outputs of organizations as important for effective management, recent research indicates that strategic control of human resources is also important.

Theory at a glance:

According to control theory, individuals having personal control are able face difficult moment with poise and experience less stress as opposite to individuals having less personal control. Research has proved personal control enhances job satisfaction.

The other version of the theory calls for strategic control of human resources just like what traditional management view was to control inputs and outputs of the organization.

Application of the Theory to the Teaching Profession:

It would be certainly interesting to find how many teachers have personal control over their lives. The other version of the theory has called for strategic use of human resources which is absolutely important in case of teaching profession. The abilities of the teachers are sometimes found to be underutilized or over utilized. Management must ensure that the teachers have got right abilities for the job and use the abilities appropriately.

The Agency Theory:

The Agency Theory was developed on the basis of some concepts in financial economics. An agency relationship is said to exist when one or more individuals, i.e. the principal, engages another person, i.e. the agent to perform some activity on his or their behalf. The agency theory assumes that the interests of principals and agents sometimes conflict with each other. This theory is important in organizational behavior as it helps in understanding how principals (owners, board of directors, or top management) can reduce conflicts between their interests and those of agents (subordinates, middle management, or shop floor employees) by establishing rewards or incentives for agents when they achieve the desired results. Research is now providing evidence that indicates that Agency Theory is applicable in various areas of organizational behavior. These include areas such as pay for performance, compensation contracts. Agency theory helps provide insights into the complex motivation processes of managers in modern organizations.

Theory at a glance:

According to Agency theory, when the principal (who can be the owner, top management, board of directors) employs another person i.e. the agent sometimes their interest conflicts with each other. So the Principal i.e. management can reduce the conflict by providing rewards or incentives for agents when they achieve the desired results. Theory applies to areas of performance and compensation contracts.

Application of the theory to the Teaching Profession:

The theory has called for establishment of reward or compensation system for the performance of the agent for reduction of the conflict of interest. That seems to be the crux of the problem with teaching profession. The reward system is not based on performance but is based on certain number of years of completed service. There have been calls from the academic experts to make the rewards contingent upon performance in case of teacher's performance.

INTEGRATING CONTEMPORARY THEORIES OF MOTIVATION

It would have been simple if there was one Motivation theory which could have been applied in situations and in all professions. The fact that a number of these theories have been supported and criticized on many accounts only complicates the matter. But these theories are not all in competition with one another. Because one is valid doesn't automatically make the others invalid. In fact, many of the theories presented are complementary.

Performance Dimensions

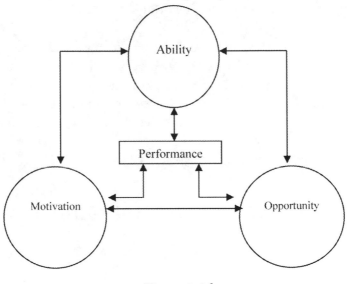

Figure 1.16

Source: Adapted from M. Blumberg and C. D. Pringle, "The Missing Opportunity in Organizational Research: Some Implications for a Theory of Work Performance", Academy of Management Review (October 1982), p.565.

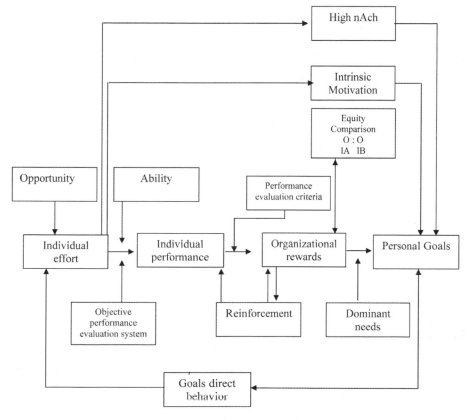

Figure 1.17
Integrating Contemporary Theories of Motivation

7 MOTIVATORS APPLICABLE TO TEACHING PROFESSION

Knowledge about the theories of motivation, though useful is not enough to motivate employees at work situations. A manager must know specific ways which could help him motivate his subordinates. It goes to the credit of organizational behavior that it has several readymade techniques and programs which can be used by the manager. The more important amongst them are money, job design participative management, quality of work life, behavior modification and others.

A. MONEY

Money is understood to be a powerful motivator for more than one reason.

- In the first place, money is fundamental for completion of a task. Work, unless it is voluntary or "play", involves a contract between two parties "guaranteed" by the payment of money. An employee takes pay as the reward for his work and the employer views it as the price for using the services of the employee.
- Second, as a medium of exchange, money is the vehicle by which employees can buy numerous need satisfying goods and services they desire.

- Third, money is one of the hygiene factors and improving maintenance factors is the first step in efforts directed towards motivation.
- Fourth, money also performs the function of a "score card" by which employees assess the value that the organization places on their services and by which employees can compare their "value" to others.
- Fifth, reinforcement and expectancy theories attest to the value of money as a motivator. In the former, if pay is contingent upon performance, it will encourage workers to high levels of effort. Consistent with the expectancy theory, money will motivate to the extent that it is seen as being able to satisfy an individual's personal goals and is perceived goals and is perceived as being dependent upon performance criteria.
- Sixth, money acts as punctuation in one's life. It is an attention getting and affect producing mechanism. Money has, therefore, tremendous importance in influencing employee behavior.
- Seventh, money is easily vulnerable for manipulation. Other factors like satisfaction, responsibility job and the like are nebulous. Payments and the plans with which they are linked are manipulatable.
- Finally, money will be a powerful motivator for a person who is tense and anxious about lack of money. Many worries and concerns are financially based. It is relaxing to receive sufficient money to clear the outstanding bills and past debts which have been causing tensions.

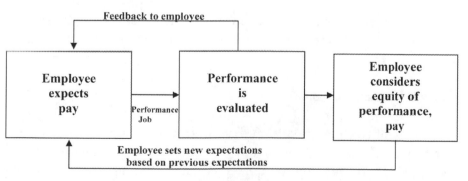

Figure 1.18

But behavioral scientists think otherwise. They downgrade money as a motivator. They prefer, instead, other techniques such as challenging jobs, goals, participation in decision making and other non monetary incentives for motivating employees. The opposition of behavioral scientists to money as a motivator is understandable for at least six reasons.

- First, money is not important to all people. High achievers, for example are intrinsically motivated. Money has little impact on the people.
- Second, people fail to see a direct linkage between monetary rewards and performance. In these days of unionization, protective legislation, seniority based promotions and the cost of living indexation, pay raises do not depend on performance.
- Third, for money to motivate the difference in pay increases between a high performer and an average performer must be significant. In practice it rarely is.
- Fourth, management must have the discretion to reward high performers with more money. This is not possible, thanks to strong unionization.
- Fifth, relationships among employees are often ruptured because of the scramble for monetary rewards.
- Finally, financial incentives discourage risk taking propensity of people. Whenever people are encouraged to think about what they will get for performing a task, they become less inclined to take risks or explore possibilities.

The conclusion is that money can motivate some people under some conditions. Put in another way, money cannot motivate all people under all circumstances.

Money & Teaching Profession

In case of teaching profession there were gross complaints on the part of teachers that their remuneration was not sufficient enough especially compared to other profession. A graduate finishing his engineering or a student who has finished his MCA would obviously prefer to join the corporate world rather than turning towards academics on account vast difference he finds between salary what he would get as corporate employee and as a teacher. Teaching profession was thus losing best talent on account of poor reward system. Some accused the lower reward system to the low status of teachers in the society. Some even went extent saying teachers' value in marriage market was so low; marrying a teacher is considered to be the last choice. Fortunately teachers are the major beneficiaries of Six Pay Commission recommendations implementation. But still there has been no incentive in terms of money for such teachers who are giving their qualitative outputs to the profession of teaching.

B. JOB DESIGN

Job design involves conscious efforts on the part of the management, to organize tasks duties and responsibilities into a unit of work in such way that meets the needs of employees and organization. The design of jobs has a critical impact on the objectives of organization and employees. Jobs that are not satisfying or are too demanding are difficult to fill. Boring jobs may experience higher turnover. For an employee, motivation and job satisfaction are affected by the match between job factors (content, qualifications and rewards) and personal needs. A thoughtful job design, therefore, can help the organization and its employees achieve their objectives.

Poorly designed jobs, on the other hand, may lead to lower productivity, employee turnover, absenteeism, complaints, sabotage, unionization, resignations and other problems. It was Herzberg who conceived job design as an important instrument to motivate employees.

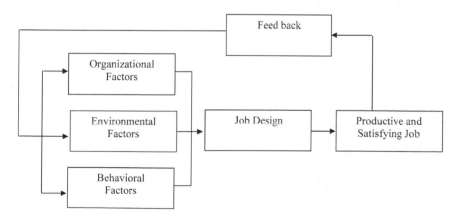

Fig. 1.19 Factors Affecting Job Design

Job Design & Teaching Profession:

The job design in case of teachers' job needs to be seriously looked into. Some teachers complain about their jobs as being boring and monotonous of conducting lectures one after another. The word lecture has become synonymous with boredom. Management should try to make job of a teacher more interesting by providing conducive organization environment and designing a good system of feedback and performance appraisal and linking performance and creativity of a teacher to reward system. Today one can hardly find any connection between performance and pay in teaching profession. Plus as the teacher progresses from one position to other i.e. from the position of lecturer to the position of Assistant Professor or Professor, one would hardly find any difference between their previous job duties and responsibilities apart from reduction in number of lectures he is supposed to conduct. The job design remains almost same. One can also look into the aspect of changing job design as the teacher travels across the career ladder.

Job Enrichment

First coined by Herzberg in his famous research with motivators and maintenance factors, job enrichment has become a popular concept. It simply means adding a few more motivators to a job to make it more rewarding. To be specific, a job is enriched when the nature of the job is exciting, challenging and creative or gives the job holder more decision-making, planning and controlling powers.

According to Herzberg, an enriched job has eight characteristics. These features are described below and illustrated in Fig.

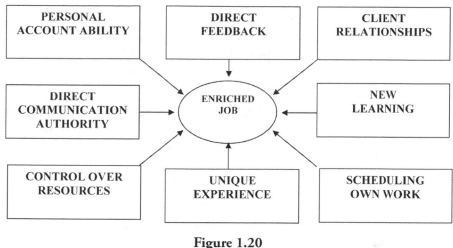

Figure 1.20
Characteristics of an enriched job

(Source: K.Ashwathappa, Organizational behavior, p. 241)

Job Enrichment & Teaching Profession

If we try to match the characteristics of enriched job with that of teacher's job, many of the characteristics are missing. There is complete lack of accountability in case of teachers. There is no formal performance evaluation system in place in case of teachers. Teachers do not get feedback for their performance. A proper system of feedback must be designed in order to let him know how he is doing. In the Indian education system there are many bureaucratic hurdles, requiring teachers asking permissions for grant of resources and a teacher find less control over his job. There is lack of autonomy and are more controls and restrictions. A teacher is supposed to be in the learning process throughout his life. But how many teachers actually upgrade their knowledge is also a serious question. Teacher's job in its originality is said to be the most enriching. It is called as "Mother of All Professions". It is the less dedicated teachers as well as bureaucratic administrative system which have dampened its enrichment.

Some Cautions about Job Enrichment in case of the Teaching Profession:

1. Job enrichment is not a substitute for good management:

Job enrichment can't be a substitute for conducive organization environment, good supervisory practices and good reward system. So unless the management is supportive and positive, no teacher will find his job interesting, even if many elements are added to enrich the job.

2. "Enriched" is a relative term:

Adding more responsibilities to job may mean enrichment. But enrichment is relative concept. For an observer the job may look enriching, but for a teacher, it still may be boring.

3. Enrichment of jobs may create a "snowball" effect:

Care must be taken that enriching one's job doesn't result in taking away responsibilities from the other person or changing the total system organizational hierarchy or rewriting job description. The teachers will certainly resist any drastic change in their duties and status.

4. Job enrichment assumes that workers want more responsibility:

One must look into satisfaction level of teachers. A teacher whose abilities are underutilized, job enrichment will work but a teacher who is already satisfied with his current level of responsibilities, may create more problems than cure.

5. Job enrichment may have negative short-run effects:

As the teacher will take time to get adjusted to new responsibilities, one may find confusion initially but afterwards, he will get used to the job.

6. Job enrichment may become static:

A person's capacities are dynamic and ever changing. So once get used to the enriched job, he may find even this job as boring because his abilities and skill are grown. So there would be more need of enrichment.

7. Participation can affect the enrichment process:

In case of teachers participation in deciding their job design can certainly have positive effect.

8. Change is difficult to implement:

Change is always difficult to implement. Until and unless teachers are taken into confidence job enrichment programs will have serious resistance from the teachers.

Job Enlargement:

Closely related to job enrichment is job enlargement. Job enlargement refers to adding a few more task elements horizontally. A typist's job is enlarged, for example, when she is asked to type 20 letters a day instead of 10 she had been typing earlier. Fig.1.21 shows the distinction between job enrichment and job enlargement. As it is clear from Figure, job enrichment focuses on satisfying higher-order needs, while job enlargement concentrates on additional tasks to the worker's job for greater variety. The two approaches can even be blended together, by both expanding the number of tasks and adding more motivators for a two-pronged attempt to improve quality of work life (QWL).

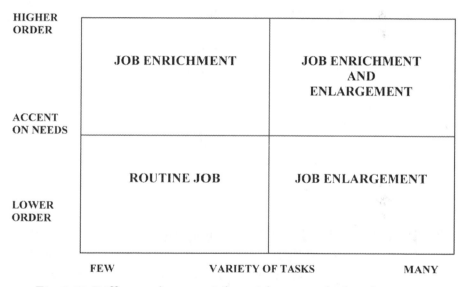

Fig. 1.21 Difference between job enrichment and job enlargement

(Source: Newstorm and Keith Davis, Organizational behavior, p. 348)

Job Enlargement & Teaching Profession

In case of teaching profession, teachers are already overloaded with the number of lectures to be taken per week in some of the private institutions. Plus additional clerical work load of preparing various reports for various committees leave less of time for research or consultancy. More than job enlargement, job enrichment should be applied to teaching profession.

Job Rotation

This involves shifting an employee from one job to another. When an activity is no longer challenging, the employee would be rotated to another job, at the same level, that has similar skill requirements. It reduces boredom and disinterest through diversifying the employee's activities. Other benefits are also available. Employees with a wider range of skills give management more flexibility in scheduling work, adapting to changes and filling vacancies. Job rotation also has drawback. Training costs are increased, work is disrupted as rotated employees take time to adjust to a new set-up and it can demotivate intelligent and ambitious trainees who seek specific responsibilities in their chosen specialty.

Job Rotation in case of the Teaching Profession:

Job rotation or what is famously known in the educational world as "Faculty Exchange Program" can be great motivators for the teachers where faculty member of one institute get a chance to teach in another institute and vice versa. It is an enriching experience to the teacher as he addresses new students and faces new environment. He gets to learn lot which goes a long way in developing his abilities as a teacher. Some of the institutes in India have got tie ups for Faculty Exchange Program with Foreign Institutes.

C. PARTICIPATION/ EMPLOYEE INVOLVEMENT:

Employee participation in management or participative management refers to associating representatives of employees at every stage of decision-making. Participation encourages and permits contributions to decisions, goals and plans along with suggestions on how these can be implemented. The motivational basis of participations is that people like to be asked their opinion and know that their ideas and beliefs have some influence in the ultimate management action taken. The underlying assumptions are people derive satisfaction from being part of the management action, from doing as effective a job as practical and from having a self-control rather than organization control.

In terms of the Two-Factor Theory, participative management could provide employees with intrinsic motivation by increasing opportunities for growth, responsibility and involvement in the work itself. Similarly, the process of making and implementing a decision and then seeing how it works could satisfy the growth needs of the ERG theory.

Participative management, however, needs to be introduced with circumspection. Best results will follow when (1) management has a large heart to share responsibilities with employee representatives; (2) employees are prepared to accept responsibilities; (3) employees have knowledge about the subject; (4) time to participate is available; (5) participants are familiar with the constraints to be observed (legal requirements, company policies etc.); (6) effective communication exists; and (7) each participate knows that personal position and status will not be adversely affected by participation.

The above conditions are rarely fulfilled. Participative management is therefore not successful in India.

Participative Management/ Employee Involvement and Teaching Profession

A teacher needs to be the owner of the entire process of passing on knowledge to the student. Right from designing the syllabus, deciding the lecture schedule, methodology of teaching, setting question paper, conducting examination, evaluating question papers and giving students feedback about their performance; a teacher should be involved in each of the process.

However what we find in India, a teacher teaches the syllabus designed by someone else which remains unchanged for years together losing its relevance to the changing times, exam papers are set by different teachers, and evaluation is made by another teacher. So a teacher has got little control over the process. A teacher should be actively involved in each part of the process.

However caution needs to be made about the conditions those are required for implementing participative management. One is that employees are ready to accept the responsibilities and the other they should have full knowledge of the subject. How many teachers have got updated knowledge regarding their subject? How many of them are in touch with industry happenings, is a real question.

(D) BEHAVIOR MODIFICATION

Organizational behavior modification (OB Mod) is yet another technique of influencing behavior of people in organizations. OB Mod uses the reinforcement principle of B.F Skinner to provide managers with a powerful and proven means for changing employee behavior. Fig.1.22 summarizes the application of OB Mod.

The steps in OB Mod are explained below:

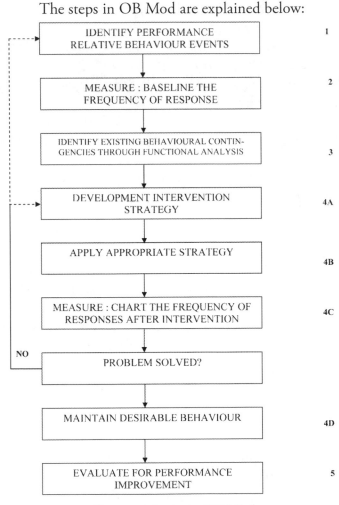

Fig. 1.22 Steps in OB Mod

(Source: "Management of Behavioural Contengencies", Fred Luthans and Robert-Krietner, Personnel, July, 1974)

Step 1—Identification of critical behaviors:

The first step is to identify the critical behaviors that make a significant impact on the employee's job performance. These are those 5 to 10 per cent of the behavior that may affect upto 70 to 80 per cent of each employee's performance.

Step 2—Measurement of the behaviors:

After behavior has been identified in step 1, they are measured. A baseline frequency is obtained by determining the number of times that the identified behavior occurs under present conditions. The purpose of the baseline measure is to provide objective frequency data on the critical behavior.

Step 3—Functional analysis of the behavior:

The goal of an OB Mod program is to increase the likelihood that people will in fact engage in the behaviors which are critical to the successful performance of their jobs. Once these critical behaviors have been identified and measured, it is necessary to determine what the causes and consequences of these behaviors are. This involves analyzing; (a) the anteceded cues: the factors which seem to instigate the behavior; and (b) the consequences, the results which accrue to the person as a result of engaging in the behavior. This process of analyzing the antecedent cues and the consequences of behavior is referred to as functional analysis in OB Mod.

Step 4—Development of an intervention strategy:

The term intervention refers to the actions that will be taken by the manager or organization in order to increase the frequency of desirable critical behavior and to decrease the frequency of undesirable behavior. This is the critical step in the process, since it is here that the manager uses the results of the first three steps to design and implement techniques to change the behavior of his subordinates. The emphasis is upon identifying rewards that can serve as positive reinforces and establishing methods of providing these reinforces contingent upon subordinates engaging in the desirable critical behaviors. Positive reinforcement is employed to increase the likelihood of desirable behavior. Negative reinforcement is used as little as possible.

Step 5—Evaluation to ensure performance improvement:

In order to determine whether an OB Mod program has achieved its desired results, it is necessary to evaluate the effects of the program in systematic and objective fashion. The results of such evaluation can be used both to determine whether the program should be continued or not and to "fine-tune" the interventions to increase their value and their ability to increase effective performance.

OB Mod in case of the Teaching Profession

OB Mod can be used in an effective way in the teaching profession to solve certain problems of absenteeism of the teachers, not engaging classes and engaging classes late than the scheduled time. The director or principal or the HoD can observe the number of times the behavior is taking place and can analyze the behavior and its causes. Accordingly he can design appropriate strategy to instigate desired behavior. However management must remember positive reinforcer will always work well in case of teachers than negative reinforcers. As the teaching community comes under highly intellectual class, any kind of action resulting in hurting self-esteem of teacher can result in drastic reaction on the part of teacher as harsh as deciding to leave the institute; there by losing a good teacher at times. Teaching is highly skilled job and seeks autonomy and freedom. Late arrivals, irregular lectures on couple of times can certainly be neglected. Too much of surveillance on the activities of the teacher should be avoided. But if the undesired action continues for long period of time then certainly OB Mod can be brought into effect.

E. QUALITY OF WORK LIFE

The term "quality of work life" means different things to different persons. For example, to a worker on an assembly line, it may just mean a fair day's pay, safe working conditions and a supervisor who treats him with dignity. To a younger new entrant, it may mean opportunities for advancement, creative tasks and a successful career. To academics it means, the degree to which members of work organization are able to satisfy important personal needs through their experiences in the organization.

There are many factors which can contribute to quality of work life. They are:

1. Adequate and fair compensation.
2. A safe and healthy environment.
3. Jobs aimed at developing and using employee's skills and abilities.
4. Growth and security of jobs aimed at expanding employee's capabilities and avoiding obsolescence of skills and knowledge.
5. An environment in which employees develop self-esteem and a sense of identity.
6. Protection and respect for employee's rights to privacy, dissert and equity.
7. A sensible integration of job career and family life and leisure time.

It would not be incorrect to say that quality of work life in fact, covers all aspects of worker's life with special reference to his interaction with his work and his working environment.

QWL in case of the Teaching Profession:

One would find a teacher leaving miserable life as far as his work life is concerned. One would also find exploitation of young talent in the form of clock hour basis payment system. The place he works, some times does not have a room for teachers to sit and eat their lunch, forget about special cabins, computers, internet. He supposed to address an over crowded classroom or a deserted classroom with very few students being present who keep on changing every day. A teacher may find complete lack of dignity the way he is treated by the management and some times by the students. Job security aspect is also missing at times when they are recruited on contract basis especially in case of privately owned colleges. There are no rewards for good performance. He works in an environment which is spoiled with politicization, nepotism, corruption, manipulation and there is hardly any motivation for growth and advancement.

Quality of Work Life certainly needs to be improved in case of teaching community.

F. OTHERS

1. MBO

The other motivational techniques used in organizations to influence employee behavior include Management by Objective (MBO), flexible working hours, two-tier pay system, flexible benefits and the like. The key of MBO is that it is a participative process, actively involving managers and subordinates at every organizational level. Propounded by Peter F. Druker in 1954, MBO, has motivational potential because the participants become ego-involved in decisions they have made. They tend to accept the decisions as their own and feel personally responsible for implementing them.

In case of teaching profession also MBO can work well where the teacher and the concerned Head of Department can set the goals for the academic year, actively involving the teacher and also the parameters to be used for evaluating the performance of the teacher. At the end of a particular time period, both can again sit together to relook at the performance and find out ways to improve if it is not upto the mark.

2. Flexitime

A system of Flexible Working Hours, which is also called flexitime, to suit the convenience of individual employees has often been pointed out as one of the techniques of motivation. Various work weeks are being used, all with the aim of lengthening the leisure between work periods. Most common are the five-day 40 hour week with two days off (5/2), the three day, 36 hour week with four days off (3/4) and the seven-day, 70 hour week with seven days off (7/7). Of these the 5/2 arrangement is highly popular.

The benefits claimed for flexitime are numerous. They include reduced absenteeism, increased productivity, reduced overtime expenses, a lessening in hostility towards management, elimination of tardiness and reduced traffic congestion around work sites. In terms of motivational theories, flexitime corresponds to the diverse needs of the work force. It appeals to an individual's growth need (ERG theory) or desire for autonomy (motivation hygiene theory).

Flexitime is the concept introduced to lengthen the leisure between work periods. Teachers have got ample of such time after completing his lectures of the day. Plus a teacher demanding complete autonomy in case of time can join as a visiting faculty to take classes according to his convenience. Plus the scheme of 2nd and 4th Saturday holiday is also applied in many government aided colleges. Some private institutes are keeping Saturdays off for teaching, making faculty members possible to spare time for research or preparation of lectures in the coming week.

Two-tier Pay System:

This provides for offering significantly lower wage rates to newly hired employees than those already employed in the same job. The two-tier pay system is seen everywhere in organizations. A junior lecturer in a university is paid less than a senior grade lecturer. Similarly, a worker in a factory with 15 to 20 years of experience is put on a higher scale than a beginner.

The Two tier payment system is said to be a kind of loyalty bonus to those members of the organization who have remained with it for considerable amount of time. But sometimes the equity theory of motivation can make a new comer compare his payments with the senior faulty member feel injustice that he is paid less for the same or even more work done by him. But these are the realities of the teaching profession. What needs to be done is that payment should be made performance based and for the reason a good system of performance evaluation must be applied that the good performer whether young or old gets well paid for his work.

Flexible Benefits:

These allow employees to pick and choose from among a menu of benefits package that is individually tailored to his or her needs and situations. The program seeks to replace the traditional fringe benefits program which applies uniformly to all employees. The idea of flexible benefits operates on the following lines.

An organization sets up a flexible spending account for each employee, usually based on some percentage of his or her salary and then a price tag is put on each benefit. Options might include inexpensive medical plus with high deductibles; expensive medical plus with low or no deductible; hearing, dental and eye coverage, vacation, vacation options, extended disability a variety of savings and pension plans; life insurance; college tuition reimbursement plans and extended vacation time. Employees then select benefit options until they have spent the amount in their respective accounts.

Consistent with the expectancy theory thesis that organizational rewards should be linked to each individual employee's goals, flexible benefits individualize rewards by allowing each employee to choose the compensation package that best satisfies his current needs.

In case of teaching profession also, pensions, provident fund, medical allowances, lean programs, paid leaves are applied. Plus the privately owned institutions are coming up with attractive reward packages like performance based increments; paid holidays, zero percent loan for purchasing laptops or computers, special allowances for conducting extra classes, special allowances for working on Sundays etc.

EMPLOYEE RECOGNITION PROGRAMS

What Are Employee Recognition Program?

Employee Recognition Program consists of personal attention, expressing interest, approval and appreciation for a job well done.

Linking Recognition Program and Reinforcement Theory

Consistent with reinforcement theory, rewarding a behavior with recognition immediately following that behavior is likely to encourage its repetition. Recognition can take many forms. One can personally congratulate an employee in private for a good job; send a handwritten note or an e-mail message acknowledging something positive that the employee has done; for employees with a strong need for social acceptance, one can publicly recognize accomplishments. To enhance group cohesiveness and motivation, one can celebrate team success.

In teaching profession also some institutes do reward their best performing teachers by giving them "Best Teacher" award. In India Teachers' Day is celebrated on 5th September every year. Such awards are given on this day. A teacher also finds complements for his work in weekly held meetings where the HoD can appreciate the performance which can encourage other teachers. However many teachers especially in government aided institutions complain about not having any recognition for the work done by them.

What Are Skill-Based Pay Plans?

Skill-based pay is an alternative to job-based pay. Rather than having an individual's job title define his or her pay category, **skill-based pay** (also sometimes called competency-based or knowledge-based pay) set pay levels on the basis of how may skills employees have or how many jobs they can do.

From management's perspective flexibility, filling staffing needs is easier when employee skills are interchangeable. Downsized organizations require more generalists and fewer specialists. While skill-based pay encourages employees to acquire a broader range of skills, it facilitates communication across the organization because people gain a better understanding of others' jobs. Where skill-based pay exists, one is less likely to hear the phrase, "It's not may job!" In addition, skill-based pay helps meet the needs of ambitious employees who confront minimal advancement opportunities. These people can increase their earnings and knowledge without a promotion of a job title. Finally, skill-based pay appears to lead to performance improvements.

What about the downside of skill-based-pay? People can "top out"—learning all the skills the program calls for them to learn. This can frustrate employees after they've become challenged by an environment of learning, growth and continual pay rises. Skills can become obsolete. When this happens, what should management do? Cut employee pay or continue to pay for skills that are no longer relevant? There is also the problem created by paying people for acquiring skills for which there may be no immediate need. Finally, skill-based plans don't address the level of performance. They deal only within issue of whether or not someone can perform the skill.

Linking Skill-Based Pay Plans to Motivation Theories

Skill-based-pay plans are consistent with several motivation theories. Because they encourage employees to learn, expand their skills and grow, they are consistent with ERG theory. Among employees whose lower-order needs are substantially satisfied, the opportunity to experience growth can be a motivator.

Paying people to expand their skill levels is also consistent with research on the achievement need. High achievers have a compelling drive to do things better or more efficiently. By learning new skills or improving the skills they already hold, high achievers will find their jobs more challenging.

There is also a link between reinforcement theory and skill-based-pay. Skill-based-pay encourages employees to develop their flexibility to continue to learn to cross-train to be generalists rather than specialists and to work cooperatively with others in the organization. To the degree that management wants employees to demonstrate such behaviors, skill-based-pay should act as a reinforcer.

In addition, skill-based pay may have equity implications. When employees make their input-outcome comparisons, skills may provide a fairer input criterion for determining pay than factors such as seniority or education. To the degree employees perceive skills as the critical variable in job performance, the use of skill-based pay may increase the perception of equity and help optimize employee motivation.

In case of teaching profession skill based plan can be applied whereby a teacher who can teach or has got qualification in diverse areas can be paid more accordingly. It will also encourage the teachers to get qualified in other areas also. It can help the institute reduce the dependence on visiting faculty; sometimes it is difficult to find good visiting faculties. The same work can be done by in house faculty. Suppose a management teacher with HR specialization acquires degree in law, his compensation can be increased considering that he can be used for teaching some of the legal aspect related subjects. Or may be a marketing specialist faculty member acquires a degree in International Business or Economics, payment can be upgraded since he is more qualified and can fit to teach different subjects. It will encourage teachers to continue learning and acquiring knowledge process. Therefore instead of paying teachers on the basis of seniority, skills and knowledge in different areas can be the criteria for increments. It can also reduce the perceived feeling of inequity as the teacher will perceive skill and diversified knowledge areas as a critical variable in job performance.

Theories which are most relevant to the Teaching Profession

1. Herzberg's Two Factor Theory
2. McGregor's Participation Model Theory
3. Achievement Motivation Theory
4. Murray's Manifest Needs
5. Equity Theory
6. Cognitive Evaluation Theory
7. Goal-Setting Theory
8. Hackman-Oldham Job Characteristics Model
9. A Model of Intrinsic Motivation
10. Attribution Theory
11. Control Theory
12. The Agency Theory

8 PROPOSED MOTIVATION THEORY APPLICABLE TO THE TEACHING PROFESSION

Diagrammatic Representation of the Theory

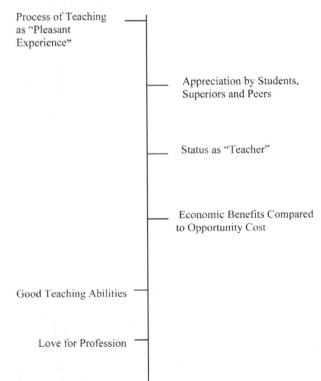

Intrinsic Factors   **Extrinsic Factors**

Process of Teaching
as "Pleasant
Experience"

                                         Appreciation by Students,
                                         Superiors and Peers

                                         Status as "Teacher"

                                         Economic Benefits Compared
                                         to Opportunity Cost

Good Teaching Abilities

Love for Profession

Love for the Profession: It has been classified as "Intrinsic Motivation Factor" which gives motivation to the individual from within. It is the first and basic obligation for being in the profession. The teacher entering this profession firstly must have love for the profession. The love should come from within. The recruitment and selection procedure for the teacher should be improved substantially. The idea of establishing "Selection Commission for the Teachers" has been propagated by many eminent educationists. The commission should work on the same ground just as UPSC (Union Public Service Commission) which has got an elaborate selection procedure for selecting officers like that for the post of IAS where a candidate goes through many challenging screening procedures. The first thing which should be looked into whether the candidate has got interest for the profession or he is opting for the profession as choice or compulsion. For being motivated in the profession, a candidate should have love for the profession at the first place itself. Another motive should be traced in the candidates is that of achievement because these are the people who would prefer challenging job with less pay over simple job with more pay. Teaching profession is in dire need of such candidates who have love for the profession and have strong achievement motive in them. A candidate who has entered the profession as the last option will keep being frustrated in the profession. Neither he will enjoy his job nor will be able to contribute anything positive to the profession. Infact he will prove to be the liability for the profession.

Good Teaching Abilities: Mere love for the profession will not prove to be adequate. The candidate should have complimentary skills to contribute to the profession impressively. A teacher should have good teaching abilities which include updated knowledge, good communication skills and empathy towards students' intellectual abilities. This is the only way a teacher can establish himself as "Good Teacher" or "Excellent Teacher" in front of the students. It is always said "Respect should not be demanded; it should be commanded". Let him be the most dumb student, he surely has the abilities to judge the teacher as bad or good. It's only the good teaching abilities which command respect for the teacher; no other gimmick is going to work for the teacher for proving himself. It is the knowledge and the way in which he passes on the knowledge to the students, will determine his teaching abilities. Many of the times it has been found teachers do have knowledge and intellectually an excellent teacher. However he does not have the necessary communication skills required to pass on that knowledge. So it's important to have good communication abilities. While doing all this, a teacher should be able to understand the intellectual abilities of his students. Teacher should keep on seeking feedback through different ways like asking questions and carrying on different tests. He should be able to bring himself to the level of students' intellectual abilities. It would be then the students will get what the teacher is trying to convey. There can't be any excuse for not being able to match to students' abilities. It is the real teaching skill. These are the teachers' who are respected not during the course time but they are also remembered by students through out their life.

The Economic Benefits: Extrinsic motivation is the motivation which is provided externally for better performance. The teachers should get economic benefits at par to his opportunity cost; something as student he would get had he opted for some other profession. One of the facts must be taken into account without being hypocritic. Gone are the days where teachers were *rishis and munis* (saint and sages). They did not have any economic expectations. On the other hand, they would provide all the facilities like food, shelter to the student. In today's times where the societal values itself are turning more and more materialistic, asking teachers to be saint and sages is not realistic. After all, the army runs on full tummies. It is not the case the students do not want to be teachers. Many of them go abroad and turn out be excellent and renowned academia. It is the environment, opportunities but also the economic benefits they get abroad are much higher than what teachers get in India. The economic benefits in India are less compared to developed world. A student passing out has got ample industrial jobs openings for him fetching more lucrative economic benefits. Plus teaching profession ask for more qualification; minimum of Post graduation (however in case of Engineering courses AICTE has brought down qualification to degree level). Given a chance to join a teaching job and corporate job, most of the students seem to be giving preference to corporate jobs, seeing whopping economic benefits corporate jobs can bring. Teaching profession still needs to offer better economic benefits to attract the cream of talent of the nation. Teaching is considered to be mother of all profession. It is essential to get talented people into it for enriching knowledge in all the professions.

The economic rewards would include monthly salary, economic incentives for good performance, substantial annual increments, after retirement benefits, so that a teacher does not need to worry for his old age times. Fortunately, teachers also are the major beneficiaries of 6th Pay Commission recommendations. The private institutes should also offer the same benefits. Many of the big private education groups infact since many years are offering more economic benefits compared to their counterparts in government sector. (However these are the groups huge in economic resources supply). Economic rewards do form an important part for teachers' motivation in today's materialistic world.

Status of "Teacher": Management must understand a teacher is the valuable HR on the basis of which the institute keeps running and earns itself respect. A teacher must be treated with atmost respect. Sufficient infrastructural support must be provided to teachers. Proper and good looking arrangement for sitting (good cabin or cubical) proper ventilation, hygienic fresh room, clean and noise free classrooms, personal computer, access to internet must be made available to teachers. In the institute where a teacher hardly have a proper place to sit, but a librarian has an air-conditioned cabin, teachers will definitely find his esteem being undermined.

A teacher should be treated as a "teacher" who should be given all the desired respect by the bosses and the management too. He should not be made to do works which undermine his self-esteem. No where in the process teacher should be dealt in a harsh manner, as this field being completely intellectual based, the egos run very high among teachers. A slight misuse of word may make a good teacher leave the organization which will result in losing valuable HR. It should always be remembered that when an employee leaves an organization, he does not leave the organization but he leaves his boss. Teaching is a kind of profession where a teacher must be self directed and self controlled and accountable to himself first for his duties. A genuine teacher needs and likes autonomy for applying creativity. Any kind of coercion will not result in positive results. The crux of the problem is recruiting those candidates who have genuine love for teaching profession. There is no need of any kind of control for self-directed teachers. Autonomy is the answer where teachers should be given all the opportunity to grow reducing his burden of administrative duties and allowing him to carry out enriched work.

Appreciation by Students, Superiors and Peers: An influential and controversial approach to influencing human behavior is based on the observation that the consequences of an individual's behavior in one situation influence that individual's behavior in a similar situation in future. Techniques based on this principle have been developed to change human behavior. Such a technique, generally known as "operant conditioning", has been advocated by B.F. Skinner. Its implication is that individual behavior can be predicted, from a person's past experiences. The operant conditioning approach to behavior is based on the law of effect, which states that behavior which has a rewarding consequence is likely to be repeated.

If a teacher is good in his performance obviously he would be appreciated. Maslow emphasized that the healthiest self-esteem is based on earned respect from others rather on fame, status or adulation. Esteem is the result of effort—it is earned. Hence, there is a real psychological danger of basing one's esteem needs on the opinions of others rather than on real ability, achievement and adequacy. Once a person relies exclusively upon the opinions of others for his own self-esteem, he places himself in psychological jeopardy. To be strong, self-esteem must be founded on one's actual worth rather than on external factors beyond one's control. It is essential, teacher should not solely depend upon the opinion of others. But it can certainly work as icing on the cake if a teacher is appreciated for his performance. Rewarding desirable behavior can definitely prove to be effective.

Process of Teaching as "Pleasant Experience": A key element of the Flow Experience is that its motivation is unrelated to end goals. The activity people are pursuing when they achieve the timelessness feeling of flow comes from the process of the activity itself rather than trying to reach a goal. So when a person experiences flow, he or she is completely intrinsically motivated. Do people typically feel happy when they're experiencing flow? The answer, which might be surprising, is No. They're too consumed in deep concentration. But when the flow task is completed, and the person looks back on what has happened, he or she is flooded with feelings of gratitude for the experience. It's then that the satisfaction received from the experience is realized. It is the desire to repeat the experience that created continued motivation. A clearer understanding of flow has been offered in Ken Thomas's model of intrinsic motivation. This extension of the flow concept identifies the key elements that create intrinsic motivation. Thomas describes employees as intrinsically motivated when they genuinely care about their work, look for better ways to do it, and are energized and fulfilled by doing it well. As with flow, the rewards an employee gets from intrinsic motivation comes from the work itself rather than from external factors like increases in pay or compliments from the boss.

A teacher too should get the same pleasure in the process of teaching. This pleasure is some thing more than job satisfaction. This pleasure is something immeasurable, unquantifiable and beyond material value. It is at this point, the teacher is at the peak of his motivation.

Conclusion

In case of Teacher motivation intrinsic factors has got more important than extrinsic factors. The first thing which must be ensured the candidates entering the profession enter the profession on account of their love for the profession.

No control, no admonishment, reminders, memos, notices can make a teacher improve his performance. It at times may boom rang; as stifled or too much controlled environment would make a teacher lose his autonomy in which he would find himself suffocated. Then the obvious question would arise, how to maintain discipline? The answer is teacher only. He/she himself/herself must realize his duties and responsibilities and should see that there is no harm being made to his image as a "teacher". This "self-realization" should come from within, that's the reason only those who love teaching profession should enter into it.

Finally, it can be concluded that a teacher reaches peak level of motivation where he is able to enjoy and get the pleasure of being involved in the vary process of teaching without being bothered for the rewards. An example can be quoted here. A pleasure something *Lata Mangeshkar* would enjoy while singing or *Sachin Tendulkar* gets in playing cricket. This pleasure would be something which can't be measurable or quantifiable.

BOOKS

1. K. Ashwathappa, *Organization Behaviour—Text, Cases, Games, 5th Revised Edition*, Himalaya Publication House, pp 189-256
2. Fred Luthans. *Organization Behavior, 10th Edition*, McGraw Hill International Edition, pp 227-267
3. Stephen Robbins. *Essential of Organization Behavior, 9th Edition*, Prentice Hall of India, pp 154 to 208
4. P.K. Agarwal, *Organization Behavior*, Pragati Prakashan, Meerut, pp 194 to 217
5. Kamala Tripathi. *Differences between Effective and Ineffective Teachers*
6. P.G. Aquinas, *O.B.—Concepts, Realities, Applications and Challenges*, Excel Books Publications, pp 95 to 128
7. Hellriegel Slocum Woodman, *Organization Behavior, 9th Edition*, Southwestern Publication, pp 128 to 162
8. Steven L McShane, May Ann, Von Glinow, Radha Sharma, *Organization Behavior*, Tata McGraw Hill, pp 152 to 176
9. Uma Sekharan, *Organization Behavior—Text and Cases*, McGraw Hill Companies, pp 63 to 90
10. John Miner, *Organization Behavior—Foundations, Theories & Analysis*, Oxford University Press, pp 133 to 244
11. Robin Fincham, Peter Rhodes. *Principles of Organization Behavior—4th Edition*, Oxford Press, pp 191 to 230
12. Kavita Singh, *Organizational Behavior—Text and Cases*, Pearson, pp 138 to 170